Tomorrow Is Today

TOMORROW
IS
TODAY

SHELLEY BRUCE

THE BOBBS-MERRILL COMPANY, INC.
Indianapolis/New York

Published by The Bobbs-Merrill Co., Inc.
Indianapolis/New York
Manufactured in the United States of America
First Printing
Designed by Jacques Chazaud

Library of Congress Cataloging in Publication Data
Bruce, Shelley.
    Tomorrow is today.
    1. Bruce, Shelley. 2. Actors—United States—Biography. 3.
Leukemia in children—Biography.
I. Title.
PN2287.B727A37 1983   792'.028'0924 [B] 83-3797
ISBN 0-672-52756-1

For Yolanda Perry,

who continues to live in the hearts
of everyone she touched.

I want to offer a word of thanks to Pam Proctor,
who helped me organize my thoughts
and get my story on paper.

ACKNOWLEDGMENTS

My life has been filled with love and support from so many people that it's impossible to mention them all. But I would like to take this opportunity to give thanks to a few of those who touched my life in very special ways:

Dr. Lee Salk and Bill Adler, who encouraged me to write this book.

The staff of Memorial Sloan-Kettering Cancer Center, especially: the pharmacists, Marvin, Paul, Mitch, and Tony, who kept me smiling in and out of the hospital; the pediatric nurses, for always being there; Dr. Naomi Hoffman, for caring enough to help; Dr. Shailesh Shah, who always kept me in stitches; and the staff of the pediatric day hospital, for making the clinic not so clinical.

Monsignor O'Brien and Father Kunz, for keeping me in their prayers; Aunt Speranza, who always keeps a watchful eye on me; Auntie Anne Root, for her love and kindness; Uncle Mickey, for always caring; Jimmy Tarzia, for never giving up; Michele Ryan and Pat Stanlaw, my beauticians, for all their special help; Dr. Wilbur J. Gould, Harry Hamburg, Martin Burden, Gene Shalit, and Bill Boggs for always letting friendship come first; the media for presenting such a delicate situation in such a hopeful and optimistic light; and the faculty of Becton Regional High School, for making it possible for me to graduate with my class in June of 1983.

My fans, for not giving up.

My doctors, Ingeborg Hoffman and M. Lois Murphy, who guided me with truth, understanding, and love.

And most of all, my family, who have given me the strength, courage, and joy to live not for tomorrow—but for today.

CONTENTS

Tomorrow Is Today

PART ONE

Will the Sun Come Out Tomorrow?

By the time I was thirteen, I had it all.

I had just finished a year's run in the title role of *Annie* on Broadway and was flush with the excitement of success.

In the two years since *Annie* had opened with a gala preview at the Kennedy Center in Washington, I had been riding the crest of a wave. I had started out in the show as Kate, one of the six orphans who lived with Annie in the orphanage run by mean Miss Hannigan. But even though my role was relatively minor, the opportunity to be in a hit show was a heady experience. In Washington we were treated like royalty. We performed at the White House and later were invited back to 1600 Pennsylvania Avenue a few times for some offstage play with Amy Carter.

But for me, that was just the beginning.

The Applause Begins

A year later, when the show's star, Andrea McArdle, got too big for the Annie role, I was picked to replace her. With my name in lights on a Broadway marquee, I suddenly found myself at the center of a whirlwind. I was hounded by autograph hunters, besieged by the press, and featured on TV shows and at charity balls. On top of all that, there were nightly dinners before the show at the famed Gallagher's steak house, where the maître d' had my table ready and the prime ribs waiting the minute I walked through the door. My performances were punctuated by backstage visits from celebrities like Burt Reynolds, who picked me up, gave me a great big bear hug, and made me feel like the most important star in the world.

All this attention and glamour didn't die down later either, even after I left the show in March 1979.

By then I was a teenager and had literally outgrown the role—my legs were too long, and I had filled out too much. But the magic of Annie continued to hold me in its spell. As a kind of perennial Annie, I appeared in a major commercial for RCA Color Track TV that was aired all over the country. In some ways, that ad brought me even more fame than my Broadway role, because now I was gaining national recognition.

Rarely a week went by without the phone ringing with a request for me to perform at a fund-raising dinner or special event. Whenever I got up on stage it was as though I had never left Broadway. In those moments I'd be swept up with the excitement of show business—the glare of the lights, the applause of the crowds, and the almost mystical turn-on that can accompany a theatrical performance. Always, I'd sing the show-stopping theme song from Annie, "Tomorrow." And always, a part of me was in that song, because I knew that my life was just beginning.

I had been at the top, but there was no reason why I couldn't go even higher. From where I stood, the future seemed to hold an endless series of sunny tomorrows, and I couldn't wait for the next day to come.

But all that changed one hot summer day in June 1981, just before the end of school. I woke up one morning with an excruciating back pain that seemed to strike out of nowhere. I complained to my mother, and she got so concerned she called for an ambulance. Before I knew what was happening, I was being rushed to the hospital, where I was checked over by several doctors who could find nothing wrong. They simply put me on codeine to kill the pain and sent me home, warning that, "If it gets any worse, come back."

Well, I didn't want to go back, but the pain continued all day long. I held out as long as I could, but then I started getting worried. Finally, by midnight that night I couldn't stand it another minute, and so my mom rushed me back to the hospital.

I was given every test imaginable to find out what was the matter. I had blood tests. I had bone-scan tests. And I had something called an IVP test for kidney function, which nearly killed me.

Before the test a nurse gave me a vial of medicine to drink that tasted like prune juice and was supposed to have the same effect. I drank about three quarters of the stuff and poured the rest down the drain. Instead of merely cleaning out my system, the stuff knocked me for a loop. I was doubled over with stomach cramps, and at one point I even passed out in the bathroom. If my mother hadn't been there to catch me, I would have cracked my head open.

I seemed to keep fading in and out of consciousness,

and as the pain grew more and more intense, I curled up in the bed in a fetal position with my thumb in my mouth. I didn't respond to anyone. The medication had left me so weak and so sick that all I could do was lie there like a baby, breathing in and out. I was also becoming more and more dehydrated, and my skin was even starting to turn brown.

The doctors insisted this was just a normal reaction to the medication. But when my aunt, who is a registered nurse, came into my room at three in the morning, she began shouting for help. "Get the oxygen," she wailed. "Can't you see this kid is dying?"

A few minutes later I was connected to the oxygen, and for several hours two nurses worked on me to ease the pain. They rubbed my stomach and massaged my back. And they got results: I couldn't stop going to the bathroom.

Back to Normal

Later that morning I got up and had the x-ray that the disastrous medicine had prepared me for, and after the test I fell into a deep sleep. When I awoke, it was as if nothing had happened. The pain was completely gone, and I felt so good that I could have walked right out of the hospital door that instant. But the doctors wanted me to stay a few more days for additional tests.

They never did find out what was wrong, and I didn't give it another thought because I felt terrific. A couple of days after I got out of the hospital, I performed at a special recital organized by my dancing teacher. Everything was apparently back to normal. I spent the rest of the summer hanging around with my friends, going to the beach, and singing at special events. After my hectic life as Annie, I found myself looking forward to another nice, normal year at school, where I could fit in to the high school scene like any other teenager.

One of the things I looked forward to most of all was being with my best friend, JoAnn Urciuoli, whom I had known since kindergarten. I had lost touch with JoAnn over the years, as I pursued my acting career, but a year after I left *Annie*, we renewed our friendship. She lived right around the corner from my home in New Jersey, and whenever she passed our house, she'd stop and talk to my mom or me or whoever was outside. Before long, she was dropping over all the time, and our friendship blossomed.

More Danger Signals

When school opened in September 1981, we found ourselves sitting side by side in many of the same classes. It was only natural then that when I began acting kind of funny in geometry class, JoAnn was the first to notice.

It was October 1, the kind of crisp fall day that should have made me feel bright and snappy. But although geometry was the first class of the day, I was already tired and strangely listless. When I tried to focus on the lesson, I found myself fighting sleep.

"What's the matter?" JoAnn whispered, as she saw my head nodding.

"I don't know," I said. "I feel achy all over. I wish I could just go to sleep."

"You'd better go to the nurse," she said. After class, JoAnn bullied me into going to the infirmary, and, finally, she escorted me there herself.

It seemed to be nothing but a very slight fever, and so the nurse sent me home. A few days later I felt well enough to go back, and for a day I was fine. By the end of the next day, though, I was running a fever again. My mom figured it must be some kind of virus, so I stayed home from school waiting for the fever to go away. When a week passed and I was still running a fever, I began to get more worried.

But my pediatrician, Dr. Ingeborg Hoffman, after checking me over and finding that my glands were swollen, put my mind at ease. "It's probably just a virus," she said. "Take this medicine, and if the fever's not gone in a couple of days, come back and I'll take some blood tests for mononucleosis."

The blood test for mono turned up negative, and although there were a few abnormal cells, there was little cause for alarm. Since I was prone to anemia, my doctor thought that maybe my anemia was acting up. To make sure, however, she sent me to a blood specialist for more extensive tests.

The Bad News

It was five P.M. on October 20 when I finished the blood workup and left the doctor's office. By the time we got home, there was a message waiting from Dr. Hoffman.

The results from the blood test were already in, she told my mother. "I want to see you tonight—at my apartment. It's up to you if you want to bring Shelley."

My mom looked at me and said, "The doctor wants to see your dad and me tonight. Do you want to come?"

The minute the question was out of her mouth, I could sense that something was terribly wrong. Whatever it was, though, I didn't want to learn about it secondhand. I wanted to be there and face it myself.

The decision to go took every ounce of courage I had in me. As we drove over to the doctor's apartment, I didn't say a word. I tried not to think about what was coming next. But I was really worried now. What's wrong with me? I asked myself over and over. Am I going to die? What does this all mean?

The closer my parents and I got to her apartment, the more anxious I became. To make matters worse, we got lost on the way to her penthouse. She lived in a new building, and it seemed as though we had to walk forever before we found the right entrance. By the time we got to her floor, we were all anxious and agitated by the whole situation, and once inside her apartment, the tension got even worse.

Dr. Hoffman greeted us warmly but her face was blank, expressionless. There was no smile on her lips that night. She graciously took our coats and motioned us to her living room, which seemed to be filled with giant plants that looked like trees. There was a big picture window with a beautiful view of the city, but even the quiet beauty of the surroundings didn't lessen my fears.

I honestly don't remember much about the conversation. All I do remember is that Dr. Hoffman sat on the floor and started talking vaguely about the blood test and how the results indicated that something was wrong, but they weren't exactly sure what it was.

As she talked, she unconsciously began to tear up paper napkins and throw the pieces on the floor. My mind was racing, trying to understand exactly what she was saying and how bad the situation was. Whatever she was trying to tell us, she was telling us so gently that nobody got the point. Or, maybe, we didn't want to understand.

Finally, my father just looked at her and said bluntly, "What do you *think* it is?"

"When they took the blood test, they found a few abnormal cells," she answered. "We won't be sure until she has some more tests. But we're 99 percent sure she has leukemia."

With that, I couldn't hold it back. I began to cry hysterically. Nothing would have consoled me, and no one really tried. Everyone was so shocked they didn't know what to do. My mom was crying, and my father's face was drawn with tension. Dr. Hoffman kept saying over and over again, "I wish it didn't have to happen. I can't understand."

I kept on sobbing as Dr. Hoffman explained to my parents what would come next. "I made an appointment for Shelley to be admitted to Memorial Sloan-Kettering Cancer Center tomorrow morning," she said. "Don't wait another day.

"If something like this happened to my own kids," she said, "I could send them anyplace in the world for treatment. But this is the best there is, and this is exactly where I'd put them."

She had done her best, but even her best gave me little assurance about the future. Nobody had the answers to the disease. "We don't know why it happened," she had said. "I'm sorry."

She drew us a map of the hospital and told us how to get in and which elevators to use. Then, we said goodnight and walked in dazed silence to the car.

What Tomorrow?

So, that was what the future held. That was the shape of my own personal tomorrow. I was sixteen years old, with what I had hoped would be a full, exciting life ahead of me. But tomorrow I'd be walking into the most famous cancer hospital in the world to be treated for leukemia. Maybe—and I couldn't even fathom the meaning of this— maybe I'd never come out.

During the ride home, we all continued in our solemn silence. My mom didn't talk. My dad didn't talk. And I didn't say a word, either. There really was nothing to say.

What could anyone say in a situation like that? Do you say, "tomorrow you're always a day away"—when tomorrow holds not the promise of hope and joy and life but the prospect of leukemia, cancer, and death? That was the litany that was running through my mind: leukemia, cancer, death.

A Bad Night

I couldn't even cry anymore. I was too stunned to cry. When I got home, my best friend JoAnn was there with my brother, Jimmy. But I didn't tell her what had just happened.

A few minutes later she said brightly, "I'll see you tomorrow." And I said, "Yeah, so long."

I couldn't bring myself to tell her face to face. A little while later, I called her on the phone. I tried to tell her, but I couldn't get the words out. I tried and tried, but the words wouldn't come. "I have to tell you something," I said. "Hold on." While she waited, I cried and cried and then came back to the phone to try again.

"I won't see you tomorrow," I said, but my voice wouldn't work. "Hold on," I whispered haltingly. And then I cried some more. Finally, I managed to blurt out, "I'm going into the hospital." Then I got my mother to talk to her, and she broke the news.

That night, I couldn't sleep. I stayed up until dawn, doing puzzles, eating, and playing Atari, until I couldn't keep my eyes open anymore. My family stayed up in shifts to keep me company, but still, we never talked about "it." As the sun peeked over the horizon, I finally dropped off to sleep for about twenty minutes.

At seven o'clock my mom woke me up and put me in the car with the suitcase she had packed. It was a cold, dreary day, and I was all bundled up in my fur boots. I slept the whole way into New York City, but that didn't refresh me. I felt as though I was sleepwalking when we went through the doors of the hospital.

A Scary Place

Dr. Hoffman had told us to take the elevators at "Bank C" to the fifth floor of the Pediatric Day Hospital, where I would be given a battery of tests and a preliminary workup before being admitted to the hospital. It seemed to take forever to find Bank C. Strange hospitals are such cold, disconcerting, scary places. But we finally found it, and my mom and I just stood there looking at each other, not saying a word.

Nurses in white were rushing all over the place. The clinic was packed with young people like me, waiting to be admitted, and others who were there for monthly chemotherapy treatment as outpatients. Somebody had taken great pains to make the clinic appear bright and cheery, with posters and rainbows of color on the wall. But the rainbows and the color and the sunlight streaming through the windows couldn't change the way I felt. I was scared, more scared than I had ever been in my life.

I didn't want to look at anything or anybody in there. Out of the corner of my eye, I caught glimpses of other kids, many much younger than I, who were sick and crippled. Some were maimed, others had lost their hair, still others were confined to wheelchairs. In the back of the clinic I could see a few kids lying in beds, with their arms hooked up to intravenous tubes. But what really frightened me was the way they looked. Some were nearly bald, like some sort of condemned prisoners, and it was impossible to tell without staring at them who was a boy and who was a girl.

Is that what will happen to me? I wondered. I could

feel my stomach tighten at the thought, and I couldn't bear to look around the room. I didn't want to search their faces for some positive sign. I thought there was nothing around me but gloom and sorrow. So I just kept my head down, staring at the floor for an hour or so, until my name was called.

Meeting the Doctor

One of my physicians at Memorial was Dr. M. Lois Murphy, a petite woman with graying hair, who had worked at the hospital with my pediatrician, Dr. Hoffman, many years before. Dr. Hoffman had gone into private practice, while Dr. Murphy had stayed on at Memorial, where she had become one of the preeminent pediatric cancer specialists in the country. It was thanks to this "old-girl network" that I had been able to get into Memorial at all, since referrals are usually made from physicians associated with the hospital.

Dr. Murphy tried to explain what would happen to me next. She said they would have to take samples of my bone marrow and that it was going to hurt. But her words kind of blurred together in my head. I couldn't stop crying, and I was so tired, I didn't much care about anything anymore. All I wanted to do was go home and go to sleep.

Taking Directions

But it would be a while before I saw my own bed again. Someone put me in a hospital gown and then motioned me to an examining table, where the nurses told me to lie on my side in a fetal position for the test. I turned around and saw the needle they were about to plunge into my back. It was a couple of inches long, and the minute I saw it, I was petrified.

"Don't move," the nurses ordered. "Just keep still."

Instinctively, I froze. I was so used to taking stage directions, that I responded almost automatically.

Three nurses surrounded me, and then the doctor plunged the needle into my hipbone. The minute she began to draw the marrow out through the needle, I started screaming. It felt as though my insides were being pulled out. The needle was tugging at something, and whatever it was, it didn't seem to want to come out. The bone marrow itself looks like blood, but it's all meshed together, and in drawing it out, the inside of my bone was literally being torn apart.

I was screaming and screaming as they took one vial of marrow and then another. Nothing could relieve the agony. I couldn't receive any anesthetic because the drug that could be used outside the operating room had been known to cause hallucinations in older patients. Children under twelve, however, could receive an injection of a short-term, preanesthetic, but I was too old. All I could do was try to bear the pain and hold out for as long as it took. I didn't really understand what was happening to me, and it was maddening not to know how long it would last. As a result, I tensed my body and fought back, and that only prolonged the agony.

"Oh gosh, please make it stop," I cried. By now, the three nurses and my mother were holding me down so I wouldn't move, and my mother was praying in my ear.

"Pray," she said. "Pray." But all I could do was moan and scream. When would it stop? Surely they couldn't keep going on with this?

But even after five minutes had elapsed, they still were taking more. "I think you'd better stop now," I said through my tears. "I think you'd better take it out."

Even my mother couldn't take it any more. "You'd better stop now," she said.

But they wouldn't stop. They couldn't stop until they had enough marrow to do conclusive tests.

When the ordeal was finally over, eight minutes later, I couldn't talk. I had screamed so much, I had completely lost my voice.

The Horror Was Real

The nurses put me in a wheelchair and rolled me down to another floor for a chest x-ray, and then, finally, they wheeled me to my room. I had come in, an energetic young actress on her feet, but now I was an invalid in a wheelchair, just like the other kids I had seen and felt sorry for when I first walked through those hospital doors.

It was only about noon, but to me, it seemed like the middle of the night. The blinds were drawn tight, and not a ray of sunshine broke through. My surroundings resembled a dark and dreary dungeon; they exuded a creepy sort of atmosphere reminiscent of Dracula's lair in all those horror films. But this horror was real.

In the bed next to mine was a tiny infant who was dying of the same disease that had struck me from out of nowhere. Her mother stayed with her day and night and kept the room shrouded in darkness so they could sleep whenever fatigue overcame them.

But to me, it was like being confined to a dark, dreary prison, with no way out. It seemed I was being hidden from the world in a place that was much bleaker than the most forbidding corner of the fictitious orphanage that had held Annie prisoner.

That first night, I couldn't say much. I just sat in bed, staring at the walls and listening to the breathing of the baby, Yolanda, and her mother. And I watched my own mother move about the room, getting things in order before she slipped into the bed next to mine. The only comforting thought was that Mom would be at my side, day and night, as long as I was in Memorial.

I didn't know how long I'd be there—or if I'd ever come out. I really didn't want to think about it. If this baby next to me had leukemia and was dying, what chance could there be for me? I drifted off to sleep, wondering.

The First Week

The next morning I was given another test—this time a spinal tap to test for leukemia in the central nervous system and to give a drug into the spinal canal to prevent leukemia. I was so exhausted afterward, that I fell asleep. When I woke up, my grandmother and my friend JoAnn were standing at the foot of my bed, smiling at me like two guardian angels. From then on, JoAnn never missed a day visiting me in the hospital, even though she lived in New Jersey. As far as I knew, she and my family were the only ones who knew what was happening to me, and that was just the way I wanted to keep it.

The first week I was in the hospital, I refused to answer the phone. I just didn't want to talk to anybody and have to explain. I guess I was embarrassed that I wasn't physically up to par; and I also had a feeling that if I just avoided thinking and talking about my illness, it would go away. Even my mother and I didn't discuss it openly. It was too difficult for us to talk about.

When the phone did ring, Mom would answer and then she'd turn her back and talk softly. But finally, she got fed up. She looked me straight in the eye and said, "You're answering the phone this time. I'm not answering it any more."

When I tried to protest, she said matter-of-factly, "We

have to face facts, Shelley. You have leukemia. I'm sorry, but you're going to have to say it yourself. It's just as hard for me."

Saying the Word

But I still couldn't say the word aloud. And although the phone kept ringing, I pretended to myself that my grief was a private affair.

It was inevitable, I suppose, that the breakthrough came from the outside, in the form of a beautiful bouquet. Those very first flowers were from Reid Shelton, my very own Daddy Warbucks, who had played opposite me on Broadway. It was the kind of present he would have chosen for his Annie, an elegant arrangement of tiny flowers nestled in a birdnestlike basket made of moss. Reid had simply wanted to let me know he cared.

At first, instead of cheering me up, his gift only made me burst into tears. He wasn't supposed to know. No one was supposed to know. But if Reid knew, that meant that everyone else must know too. There could be no more hiding alone in my room at Memorial, surrounded only by my family and a few close friends. My terrible secret was out, and even I had to face up to it squarely.

Now, it was my turn to reach out. I had to say that dreaded word—leukemia—out loud. My way of opening up was to pick up the telephone and call my friend Lois Nardone, whom I knew from my summers at the Jersey shore. Lois didn't know about my hospitalization, and I wanted to tell her myself.

I had spent the past summer with Lois, as I had almost every summer for as long as I can remember. My family has a bungalow down at Bradley Beach, New Jersey. On one side of us was my grandparents' bungalow, on the other lived my pal, Christopher Walter, and across from us was Lois' place. During the day, all of us kids would hang out at the beach, or we'd go fishing in the big lake in front of our house. At night we'd head for the amusement parks in a big group and have a wonderful time. As the summer fun ended and we each went back to our homes and winter routines, we carried away memories that would last a whole year until we met at the beach again and picked up just where we had left off.

That's the way it had been just a month or so before I entered Memorial. Lois and I had parted at the beach, knowing that we'd see each other again the following year. But now? Now, I was in the hospital without a clue about whether I'd even see another summer—and Lois didn't even know I was there.

Late one night, when I was sure my mom and everyone else in the room was asleep, I called Lois. I knew I couldn't make the call if anyone was listening, so I waited until about midnight. I whispered into the phone and told Lois the whole story.

"I have leukemia," I said. I was kind of choked up as I broke the news, but I managed to get out the whole story. She remained very, very quiet. I don't think she really knew what to say.

I explained to her everything I knew. The more I talked, the easier it was to keep talking. It was as though I were acting out a part—that this person I was talking about wasn't really me but someone else.

Gradually, we got off the subject of my illness and went on to other things. We even laughed a little, and I began to feel a little more normal.

A Lost Voice

Not long afterward, buoyed by my conversation with Lois, I decided to go to the empty playroom down the hall to practice my singing. Actually, I was practically *forced* into practicing by a wonderful nurse named Maureen Dwyer. She loved to sing, and she always had a joke or two to boost my spirits.

Maureen claims that she had only had one professional singing lesson in her life. Her father didn't like her voice, and he warned her, "Someday, you're going to open your mouth to sing and somebody's going to drop dead."

Undaunted, she went to a singing teacher, and he played a scale. As she sang the first scale, however, the man had a heart attack and fell over dead at the piano—at least that's the way Maureen told it.

When she told her father what had happened, he shrugged and said simply, "I told you so."

Maureen swore up and down that the story was true. In any case, her enthusiasm and sense of adventure propelled me to the playroom. My mother and I tiptoed down the hall with Maureen late one night while everyone slept, and then she unlocked the door and pushed us in.

"Get in there!" she said, "You're going to sing!"

Maureen stood outside the door, and my mother went to a deserted corner of the playroom to leave me alone to vocalize. I had brought a cassette of taped scales for background, and I put them on the playroom's tape deck.

As I started to sing, my voice was shaky, and I couldn't control it at all. Notes that had come easily before I went into the hospital just didn't seem to be there. I had brought a second tape of songs from *Annie*, but I refused to even put them on the tape recorder.

Instead, I just sat in one of the tiny playroom chairs and cried. I felt as though I had just fallen through a hole and was tumbling down, down, down, out of control.

Before I had gone into the hospital, my voice had been

at its peak. I had never worried about it. In fact, I never even *thought* about it. Whenever I sang, I just sang, and always the notes were there within my reach. Now, I couldn't hit a note. My voice was gone.

Demoralized though I was, I let Maureen and my mom talk me into going back to the playroom a couple of days later to try again. I think that down deep I didn't believe that my voice was gone. It *can't* be, I told myself. I just have to practice harder.

Once again, Maureen let me into the playroom. This time, I did a little better with the scales, and my confidence started to come back. I put on the second tape—the tape with the background music from *Annie.* As the music swelled with the opening bars to "Tomorrow," I felt the adrenalin begin to flow, much as it had every night I was on stage. But when I opened my mouth to sing, "The sun will come out tomorrow . . . " all that came out was a series of squeaks. The notes I had once reached with ease, I couldn't even hit at all. That seemed to settle it—my singing days appeared to be over. With my voice gone, the very life within me seemed to die too. Where would it end? When would it end?

I slammed the tape recorder shut and ran out the playroom door. I'll never be back here again, I thought. Never.

Show-Biz Kid

I got started in show business when I was just seven years old with a role in the movie *The Godfather.*

It wasn't exactly a role. I was an extra, and my job was to stand next to Santa Claus in front of the old Best & Company department store on Fifth Avenue in New York City. If you saw the movie today, you'd never even notice me because I was on and off so quickly.

The scene was supposed to be a cheery winter tableau, with Santa ringing his bell and me looking like a happy kid before Christmas. But, in reality, I was miserable. The day the scene was shot must have been the coldest day of the year. I had forgotten my gloves, and in between takes, I had to run into the store to keep warm. After several hours of this, I was so frozen I started to cry. My Mom actually had to put socks on my hands to keep me from getting frostbite.

On top of that, they used plastic snow and blew it in our faces with a fan. The stuff stuck all over me: on my clothes, in my eyes, and in my mouth. Between the "snow" and the cold, I thought the whole experience was horrible.

If this is what being in movies is all about, forget it, I thought. When I got home that night I found my grandmother sitting at the kitchen table, and I poured out my woes to her.

"Grandma," I wailed, "I don't think I'll *ever* do this again."

She shot an accusing glance at my mother and said, "Why did you do this to her?"

Stagestruck from the Start

But my mother really hadn't done anything. Even though I was only seven, I had done it *myself*. My dancing teacher, Dottie Locker, had suggested that I get a manager and try some professional performing, and at the time it had seemed like a good idea. Dottie had been urging my mom to get me into show business ever since I was three, when she spotted me tagging along with my brother Jimmy to his dance class. While the older kids danced, I'd stand outside the door and mimic their complicated dance routines, putting on a grand show for my mom and anyone else who would watch.

"She's so cute, she should be in commercials," Dottie told my mom. But my mother resisted, and I had to confine my performances to dance recitals.

From the very start, I loved being on stage. I was such a ham at my very first dance recital that my dad started

---

My first professional pictures for show business at age six and a half. A few months later, I landed my first role as extra in the movie, **The Godfather.** *Bert Torchia*

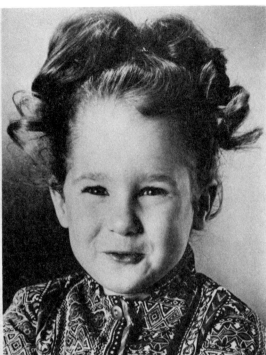

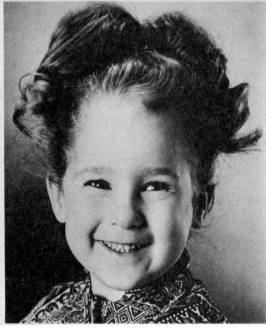

SHELLY BRUCE

Dotty Locker's School of Dance
June — Proudly Presents — 1971
— "Happy Holi-Daze" —

Dottie Locker's School of Dance in Passaic, N.J., was the place where I got my start in show biz. Here I am (second from left) at age six, looking like a chorine. When I was three, Dottie Locker told my mom, "She's so cute, she ought to be in commercials." Herman S. Paris, Photography

This is my mom's favorite photo of me, age five, dressed up as Shirley Temple in a dancing school recital. A few years later, on the Mike Douglas Show, I met Shirley Temple Black and modeled some of the clothes she wore as a child in the movies. Herman S. Paris, Photography

calling me his "little star." The show was one of those pint-sized extravaganzas where all of us kids danced and sang. Dad told me later that when all the other little girls who had leads in the show got up to sing, no one could hear them because they sang so softly and held the microphones down by their stomachs. But when my turn came, I screamed the songs as loud as I could and held the mike right by my lips. I don't know where I got such stage presence, but from that moment on, my fate was sealed.

A Try for the Big Time

It was only natural that four years later when Dottie Locker and her husband Barney suggested I get a manager and try for the big time, I started pestering my mom to let me do it. I thought it would be fun to try for something a little more professional.

It wasn't so much fun finding a manager, though, even with Barney's help. On one occasion, he drove me into New York City to audition for a prospective manager. But moments after I finished reading the script, the woman looked at Barney and said snidely, "She reads with a twitch." I was momentarily stunned, but Barney's enthusiasm helped me bounce back and keep trying until I found a manager who thought I had potential.

When the manager called to tell me about the audition for *The Godfather,* I figured, why not? I talked my mother into the idea, auditioned, landed the role, and then as I stood in the freezing cold in front of Best & Co., I found out fast that being a professional actress wasn't all it was cracked up to be.

As it happened, though, I was blessed with a very short memory. When I woke up the day after the first shooting, I said to my mom, "Let's go back." So, back we went to New York, to the plastic snow and the cold and another day of shooting.

I don't know what it was that drew me back—what mysterious force made me want to stand around waiting for cameras to roll or made me willing to keep smiling in front of Santa Claus on a cold winter's day. Certainly it wasn't because I was starstruck. I didn't even catch a glimpse of Al Pacino or Marlon Brando or any of the superstars in *The Godfather*. Anyway, I was too young to care about all of that.

Background Information

But I was old enough to sense that this world I was stepping into was somehow different from my quiet little street in East Rutherford, New Jersey. Out of curiosity, I suppose, I wanted to find out more about it.

I was born Michele Merklinghaus on May 5, 1965, and grew up in a big, rambling two-family house in a very old neighborhood. Our house was practically an antique—it was seventy years old. My mother's parents, Rose and Salvatore Pollina, lived downstairs, and I lived upstairs with my mother, Marge, my father, Bruce, and my older brother, Jimmy.

It was a crazy household, with pets of every description all over the place. We always had dogs—never just one, usually two or three—along with sea horses, ducks, and hamsters. Once I had two hamsters, which I thought were the same sex until I looked in their cage one night to find thirteen babies. What really shocked me, though, was that it looked like they were eating their babies, and I called my parents at the bowling alley where they bowled every Friday night to report on the terrible events taking place under our roof.

I don't remember a whole lot about my early life, other than the fact that there were always lots of kids and bikes in our big backyard. Also, all of the kids went either to St. Joseph's, the Catholic parochial school I attended, or to the local public schools, Franklin and Faust.

What I remember most clearly was running downstairs to my grandmother's kitchen and nibbling on her Italian specialties: stuffed mushrooms, zeppoles, and an endless stream of pies and cakes. When she was in the middle of cooking something, she'd let me help out and teach me her secrets.

For a while my great-grandmother lived in the house, too, but then she moved into a nursing home. When I was four or five I used to go up there and dance and sing for all the residents. With my freckles and brown hair done up in baloney curls, I must have looked like a miniature Annie. At any rate, the residents always gave me lots of applause and kisses, and I ate it up.

Early Auditions

With this early opportunity to be a ham, it was only natural that when I got my big "break" in The Godfather, something inside me wanted more. I began to take lessons of every kind in earnest—tap dancing, jazz dancing, ballet, and singing. My first singing teacher was a man from New York named Mr. Polanski who was great with little kids. He showed us how to do funny things with songs—such as how to use our faces and hands to dramatize our singing—and we loved it. What I loved most of all was sitting under his grand piano. Next, I moved to a singing teacher in New Jersey, Bernice Elkin. Eventually I ended up working with a terrific singing teacher in Philadelphia named Russ Faith. Every Sunday, up until the time I appeared in Annie, my parents and I would make the two-hour drive to Philadelphia for my singing lesson and turn the day into a family outing.

In order to get stage experience, I went to Tony

That's me—number 726—at age four in the Little Miss American Pageant at Palisades Park, N.J. I lost, but it didn't bother me one whit. The only thing I cared about was sliding down the amusement park's giant slide into a pile of potato sacks!

Grant's Stars of Tomorrow, where I appeared at the Steel Pier in Atlantic City and in little shows at nursing homes all over Atlantic City. At one of the homes I got to meet one of the original Ziegfeld girls, Sally Struthers, who told me all about her exciting life in the Follies. As she spoke, her eyes danced with delight, and I could tell that the thrill of show business had never left her.

Little by little I found myself looking forward to the day when I, too, would get up on stage. To move my

career along, Barney urged me to get a stage name
that would be less of a tongue twister than Michele
Merklinghaus. For a while I presented myself at auditions as "Michele Merk." But Barney still didn't like it,
and one day when my folks and I were talking with him
by the front desk of the dancing school, we brainstormed
and came up with a name that had just the right ring. It
was a combination of the nickname for Michele, "Shelley," and my dad's name, Bruce. So, as "Shelley Bruce," I
was ready to take show business by storm.

Unfortunately, for about a year after my movie debut
in *The Godfather*, I got nothing but rejections every time I
went up on an audition for a show or a commercial. But I
never really took it too seriously. I was having too much
fun just going to the auditions to worry about whether or
not I got the job. One day, for example, I got so engrossed
in a conversation with another girl who was waiting to
audition that every time the person in charge of the commercial said, "Who's next?" we'd move to the end of the
line so we could keep talking. Meanwhile, my dad was
downstairs waiting for me, circling the block in the car.
Since most commercial calls, as they are known, take
only about fifteen minutes, Dad got more and more worried as the minutes ticked by. Forty-five minutes later, I
bounced out the door with my new friend, smiling happily and still talking.

I didn't get the role in that commercial, but it didn't
really matter that much, because I knew I could always
go back and try for another. As a result, every time a
phone call came through saying that someone else got the
part, I'd just shrug it off and say, "Oh, well, maybe
tomorrow."

Pouring It On

"Tomorrow" came a year later, in the form of a commercial for Golden Griddle Pancake Syrup. Another girl had been hired for the commercial, and I was her standby. We had to get up before dawn and go to a crummy-looking studio on Tenth Avenue, in New York City, where the commercial was to be shot.

It was clear to me right from the beginning that there was nothing very glamourous about the commercial side of acting. For one thing, the places you had to work often left a lot to be desired. The studio where the pancake commercial was shot was nothing more than a gigantic ugly room where they set up lights and fixed up a set to look like a kitchen.

The personalities you encountered weren't always so pleasant, either. The director asked me to sit on the set so he could adjust the lighting, and then I took a place behind the cameras to watch the other girl eat a batch of pancakes. But, just as they were about to rehearse the scene, the girl started acting kind of obnoxious and balked at eating the pancakes and at holding up the syrup bottle. Just like that, she refused to do anything.

Before I knew it, I found myself sitting at the table in the mock kitchen, staring at a stack of pancakes, which I was only too happy to drown in Golden Griddle Syrup and eat in front of a camera.

Much later, I learned that the reaction of the other girl to doing the commercial wasn't that unusual. If you're a kid, especially one who's new to the game, it's not that easy to get up at six o'clock, hurry over to a set at seven, and then have to sit in front of some hot lights for hours and follow orders. It isn't much fun having to eat pancakes over and over again, either. And not many people get a kick out of moving a bottle of syrup from spot X to spot Y when the director gives a cue. All of this can be repetitious and boring. When you're sleepy and tired, it's hard to look on the bright side in a situation like this.

But it was easy for me to look on the bright side that

morning. After all, I was savvy enough to know an opportunity had just fallen into my lap when I was asked to replace the other girl. What's more, I *loved* pancakes. So it was sheer pleasure to be paid to eat them!

My reward, along with the money for the shooting and the residual payments every time the commercial aired, was a bottle of Golden Griddle Syrup. That night, I celebrated my good fortune by eating pancakes for dinner!

Getting It Just Right

During the next four years I made more than fifty commercials. There were TV ads for McDonald's, Peter Paul Caramello, and Swanson Fried Chicken. There were print ads for Sharp Calculators and radio commercials for the musical group Blue Oyster Cult.

Most of these were made in New York, where the ad men worked overtime to make sure every last detail was perfect. In one ad for Jiffy Pop Popcorn, I waited nearly an hour watching the advertising director pop popcorn on the stove until he got a perfect aluminum-foil bubble. Only after he had his perfect bubble could I get into the act. The scene was shot over and over until the ad was just right. During a Peter Paul candy ad, which was shot outside in a playground, the sun was so bright it was reflecting off of the candy wrappers. No matter how I held up the candy, the sun still gleamed from the wrapper. So, while I waited on the monkey bars, the crew took

My professional photo at age eight. I'm grinning because after a year of rejections, my career had begun to take off. During the next few years I made more than fifty television commercials. Bert Torchia

a special spray and dulled the outside of the wrapper so the camera could catch the name of the candy.

In a similar quest for perfection, I was flown to Florida in the middle of winter because a Stove Top Stuffing ad called for an outdoor summer scene. For a Fram Windshield Wiper commercial, I walked through a simulated rainstorm. A fire hose was pointed up in the air and the water sprayed out, falling like a cloudburst on me and a car windshield.

Once the commercials started coming my way, my life was a whirlwind. After school, I'd go up for auditions that my manager alerted me to. Almost all the auditions, with the exception of "baby calls" for infants and toddlers, were in the afternoons, and my mother would drive me to New York City to try out.

When I didn't have an audition or a shooting for a commercial, I'd continue to take performing lessons. But I don't want to leave the impression that all this training was part of some master plan my mother and I devised to catapult me to stardom by age fifteen. It was simply something I liked to do, and I took my career on a day-by-day basis as the opportunities came along.

But the more I got involved, the more I discovered that show business gave me an identity all my own. I had something that set me apart from the other kids. My career gave me a focus for my life, other than simply coming from school, doing my homework, watching TV, or playing with my friends.

After-School Work

By the time I was ten, I had already appeared in an off-Broadway play directed by the late Sal Mineo, on the *Mike Douglas Show* with Shirley Temple Black, and in a summer stock production of *The Music Man*. Those were the kinds of things that filled my life and inched me closer and closer to Broadway.

I had no idea who Sal Mineo was when I won a role in a play called *The Children's Mass*, which he directed at the Theatre de Lys in Greenwich Village. I didn't know that he was a big star. I didn't know that women had drooled over him in the movie *Exodus*, or that he was once the heartthrob of hundreds of teenagers. Luckily, too, I didn't know much about the theme of the play he was directing. It was an avant-garde story about drugs and sex; but, quite frankly, most of the dialogue in the play went right over my head.

Since I was only seven at the time, my mother had asked my pediatrician, Dr. Hoffman, and the nun who taught me in elementary school whether it was all right for me to be in the show. Both of them said that I was too young to understand the play and that they saw no harm in it.

"As long as she doesn't do anything bad on stage," said the Sister, "it's fine."

I didn't do anything bad on stage, but everyone else did. There was a lot of profanity in the show and some violence—one of the characters got killed. But Dr. Hoffman and the Sister were right. None of this had any impact on me whatsoever. In fact, I got a big kick out of watching the stagehands make fake blood backstage for the murder scene.

My grandmother, on the other hand, was mortified when she came to see me in the show. She walked out before it was over.

There wasn't too much about my role that was distinctive, but I do have vivid memories of a chair my character had to paint over and over again. I did a lot of sitting in that chair onstage, and because I was kind of jittery, I'd swing my legs back and forth. Almost every night after the show, I'd get a note from Sal Mineo saying, "Stop swinging your legs!"

Apparently, I never got the message. A few years later, when I appeared in *Annie*, the director, Martin Charnin, sent me notes on my performance that read, "Stop swinging your legs!"

It's funny how in the theatrical world certain situations and people have a way of coming back into your life again and again—just like that note on my leg swinging. One of the actors from *The Children's Mass* whom I happened to meet years later was Gary Sandy. He later became a big hit on the TV show *WKRP in Cincinnati* and also appeared in *The Pirates of Penzance*. In 1982, while he was still in *Pirates*, he showed up at the annual *Annie* party, and we had a wonderful reunion. Photographers wanted to snap our picture for publicity, but we wanted to simply be by ourselves to get reacquainted and reminisce about *The Children's Mass*.

What I remember most about the play, though, was celebrating my eighth birthday with the entire cast in Sal Mineo's apartment in Greenwich Village. He had bought a big cake and had invited everyone from the cast in as a surprise. When I walked in I saw my whole theater family standing around a cake with eight candles. I thought the party was wonderful and Sal was wonderful. But to me, he wasn't a superstar. He was just Sal Mineo.

Fun and Games

A few months later I had another brush with greatness on the *Mike Douglas Show*. Mike was interviewing Shirley Temple Black, and I was selected along with two other girls to model some of the clothes she had worn as a child in the movies. We came out, one by one, and modeled an outfit. Then we ran backstage to change into another as fast as possible so that we could get back on the set again. Things were moving at such a breakneck pace, I was afraid I might appear before the camera minus some essential article of clothing! That was my first experience at quick changes.

One thing that impressed me about Shirley Temple Black was how much fun she is. The impish sparkle in her eyes in all her movies is there even now that she's a grownup. At one point, all of us kids were sitting off camera for what seemed like hours before the show started, when she came over to us and asked, "Do you know how to play jacks?"

"How do you do that?" I asked. With that, she whipped out a set of jacks and a little ball and gave us a demonstration. She was the first person who taught me how to play the game, and I've played it ever since.

She also showed us how to do the triple time-step—a fast-paced dance step she had perfected as a child. And while we waited for Mike Douglas to call us, we triple time-stepped all over the TV studio.

It was such times that made show business great fun. Often, it didn't seem like work at all but just one big party. For example, when I appeared in a summer stock production of *The Music Man* a couple of years after the show with Shirley Temple, an actress named Spring Fairbanks, who has recently appeared on Broadway in the *Pirates of Penzance,* made the experience as much a game as a job for me.

I was only ten at the time, and I played the role of Amaryllis—the girl who takes piano lessons from Marion the librarian. During the run of the play, I kept getting secret messages attached to these funny little toy hedgehogs. The tiny animals would be left on the table in my dressing room with notes like, "Please take care of me" inscribed on them.

Every day, a different hedgehog would be left in my dressing room, but I couldn't figure out who they were coming from. The last one I received was a little girl hedgehog with a book in her hand. The note on it said, "Professor Harold Hill is a fake."

Soon after, I discovered that the hedgehogs had been left by Spring, who was playing one of the town girls. Spring's mother had given them to her, and in one of those wonderful traditions in the theater that can make this business so touching, Spring was passing them on to me. I still have them, in a special glass case all their own in my bedroom.

One of things that made show business so appealing for a kid like me was that people like Sal Mineo, Spring Fairbanks, and Shirley Temple Black always seemed to pop up just at the right time, when the job was in danger of getting boring. They added a bit of sparkle and warmth and took the edge off the hard work involved in the theater.

A Show-Biz Playmate

What made it even more exciting to be a show-biz kid was meeting all the other kids at auditions. Always, there were dozens of other girls and boys trying out for various commercials or plays, and gradually we became like a community—although our playground was the audition stage.

One of my closest show-biz playmates was a cute brunette named Andrea McArdle. Andrea and I first met when she was eight and I was seven at an audition for something called the Milliken Show. Milliken is one of the leading fabric mills, and every year as a promotion the company would put on a big theatrical extravaganza for the benefit of their Seventh Avenue clients. It was usually held at the Waldorf Astoria hotel, and had lots of singing and dancing.

Andrea and I both showed up at the Mark Hellinger Theatre for this one particular audition, and it was a typical "cattle call." Hundreds of kids were their hoping to get a chance to be in the show. For most of us, it was a long shot, a hope-against-hope that might be a step toward the Great White Way. Seventh Avenue certainly wasn't Broadway, but the Milliken Show was at least a beginning.

We were standing around with the other kids backstage, and while we waited for our names to be called to perform, we started talking and giggling about everything under the sun. Both of us made it through the dancing stage of the audition and then through the singing stage. Finally, we went up in a group wearing some of the costumes to be featured in the show.

It had been a long day, and by the costume stage we were tired of hanging around and were filled with anticipation. We had come so far that we were sure that one or the other of us was going to make it. Then they called the names of those who were chosen.

"Bradley, Brewster, Carey." I strained to hear my name, but it never came. Just as it was beginning to dawn on me that I had been rejected, they started to read off the M's, and I listened even harder to hear if Andrea had made it. "McAndrew, Murphy, Nelson."

Andrea had been rejected, too. I looked at her, and she looked at me. We burst into tears, hugging each other for solace.

It was silly to cry—we both knew that. I had been rejected for other things before, but never had my failure affected me quite the way this one had. Part of it, I think, was the way the audition was handled. On most auditions, you usually don't find out the outcome until a day or even a week later. By the time I got the bad news, I had always put it in the back of my mind and moved on to other things. If my agent called to say, "I'm sorry, you didn't get it," I'd shrug it off and look ahead to the next audition.

But the Milliken Show was different because they announced the winners right then and there. It was as if Andrea and I had been finalists in the Miss America pageant. We had gone through all the stages in the audition, only to find out immediately, at the very end, that we didn't measure up.

What made it especially hard to take was that it was announced publicly, and we both felt humiliated.

Eventually, I managed to get selected and appear in two Milliken shows, and I finally did learn how to handle the pressure. But the tension that built up every year in the Milliken audition was so great that some kids went overboard. One girl ran home after she auditioned in the morning and came back in the afternoon with her hair a different color in order to audition again. The ploy didn't work, and she was rejected twice.

Not a Typical Stage Mother

Even after Andrea and I said goodbye that first time and promised to see each other again, I cried all the way home. I tried to get my mother to comfort me by promising to take me to the circus or by buying me something special, but she wouldn't hear of it.

"If you're going to get this upset over a silly show," she said, "I'm not going to permit you to go on any more commercial auditions. It's just not that important, Shelley."

She was right, though I didn't want to admit it at the time. In fact, her whole approach to my being in show business was very relaxed and casual. Some parents would tell their kids, "If you get this, I'll be able to get that new refrigerator." Or, "You're terrific—I know you're going to get this role." But my mother was very realistic, and she'd say simply, "If you're right for the part, you'll get it, and if you're not, you won't get it. There will always be something else that you'll be perfect for."

As a result, I was never under any pressure to perform. I could go up on that stage and have some fun, and if it wasn't fun, I could put it all behind me and walk away from it.

A Deepening Friendship

Walking away from a failure wasn't always that easy to do, as I found out at the Milliken audition. But I came away from that particular audition with something much more important that any production credit I could add to my resumé. I came away with a new friend, Andrea McArdle, and our mutual disappointment somehow cemented our friendship. Over the years, our friendship grew just as it had started—not in our backyards playing with dolls like other girls our age but behind the scenes in studios and theaters where we were waiting to audition.

Oddly enough, there was never much of a sense of competition between us. Even though we might be trying out for the same role, we knew we were different types. In the first place, she was a year older than I. Secondly, she was taller, with medium-length brown hair, while I was short, with long dark brown hair. When it came to filling a role, we knew that the casting director would have a certain sense of the type of person he wanted for the part, and maybe one or the other of us just wouldn't be the right type.

So, we could relax and just enjoy the fun of being

together and sharing a "secret" lifestyle that few kids our age understood.

In a way, the day I met Andrea—even though it was something of a downer because we both got rejected for the Milliken show—was one of the most important days of my life. You see, it was Andrea who later gave me my entrée to the Broadway show which would put my name in lights.

Broadway Baby

Four years after Andrea McArdle and I met at the Milliken audition, we found ourselves sitting side by side at yet another audition—this one for a new musical called *Annie*. It was to open at the Goodspeed Opera House in East Haddam, Connecticut, in the summer of 1976.

We were both excited because the Goodspeed represented something much bigger than anything either of us had been in before. Sure, it was regional theater. But the Goodspeed was a cut above everything else. Time after time, shows from Goodspeed had gone on to Broadway. There was always a chance, even if remote, that this new show, *Annie*, might make it big, too.

Oh, To Be an Orphan

The audition itself hinted at the promise to come. It

was an "open call," which meant that everyone who was interested could show up for the audition—and everyone did. Hundreds of girls were there, trying for the chance to play Annie, the famed orphan from the *Little Orphan Annie* comic strip. Or, if that failed, they hoped for a spot as one of the six orphans who were her friends in Miss Hannigan's orphanage.

It was a long audition—about three hours—because they had so many kids to look at. The director called us up in groups and put us through our paces. First, we had to sing together. Then, we had to sing a solo of "Happy Birthday" and hit a high F sharp. Next, we were taught a few dance steps and had to hoof it on the spot. And, finally, we had to perform an improvisational routine in which we were supposed to pair up with another kid and "argue" by shouting out numbers instead of words. The idea was to rely on gestures and facial expressions to get across our mood and show how well we could act. For a grand finale, we lined up across the stage and, one by one, stomped toward the director, leaned forward with our hands on our hips, and gave him the biggest Bronx cheer we could muster. That was the fun part.

Out of this confusion the casting director was somehow supposed to zero in on the perfect Annie and six perfect orphans. It seemed like a long shot that either Andrea or I could be picked from among so many.

When I analyzed my chances, I felt I had done all right with the dancing and improvisation. But compared with some of the other kids, my singing wasn't as strong as it could have been. I blew it on the F sharp in "Happy Birthday," and deep down inside, I knew at that point I wasn't going to make it.

I was right. A few weeks after the audition, I got a call from Andrea. "I made it!" she said excitedly. She told me she had been picked to play one of the orphans, while a terrific actress named Kristin Vigard had been chosen for the title role.

That's when I knew I had been passed over. In this business, you're never called if you've been rejected; only if you've been chosen. You have to get the *bad* news through the grapevine from friends. As happy as I was for Andrea, I was down in the dumps because I wanted to be with her, sharing in the fun. The show was going to be wonderful—I could just tell—and I wanted to be part of it.

It was small consolation that when *Annie* opened a few months later, the reviews were less than enthusiastic. But to my way of thinking, successful or not, the show was filled with a bunch of happy kids who were having a darn good time.

A Break for Andrea— and One for Me

Andrea was having the most fun of all. Then, lightning struck for her: Just two weeks after the show opened, the script was changed, the cast was switched around, and overnight Andrea became Annie. The director wanted Annie to be a little toughie, and Andrea, at thirteen, seemed to have the gutsy streak he preferred.

Every now and then, I'd get a phone call from East Haddam, with an excited Andrea filling me in on all the goings-on behind the scenes. She told me how director Mike Nichols had been in the audience the first night she appeared as Annie and about the incredible response of the audience to the show. Every night there were standing ovations—cheers and applause that never seemed to stop. I would have given my right arm to be there, and in fact that's what it took to get me to East Haddam—a broken arm.

In the middle of August, just as the summer was

beginning to drag, I broke my arm skateboarding at the Jersey shore, and I found myself moping around the house with little to do. A few commercials, including one with my broken arm, did help a little to pick up my spirits. A few weeks before my accident, I had done a commercial for Bazooka Bubble Gum. The ad agency wasn't satisfied with it and wanted to reshoot it, so I had to appear—broken arm and all—for the reshoot. It took twice as long as usual to complete because they had to shoot all the camera angles to avoid the cast on my arm.

When Andrea heard about my arm, she decided to try cheering me up. "Why not come up here for a while?" she asked.

An Inside Look

I took off for Connecticut the very next day, and for the next two weeks I hung around the Goodspeed with Andrea, soaking up the excitement of this play—which everyone but the critics seemed to love. She gave me a royal welcome and introduced me to everyone connected with the show, including the director, Martin Charnin, who had come up with the idea for *Annie* back in 1972.

It was a thrill just to be there talking to people and getting an inside look at how a show like this gets started. I learned that Martin had conceived the show after running across a book of *Little Orphan Annie* comic strips. He then got Thomas Meehan to write the book, Charles Strouse to compose the music, and Charnin himself wrote the lyrics. Putting the show together wasn't quite as easy as all that, however. At first, Meehan, a humorist who had written for television and for the *New Yorker*, thought *Annie* was a dumb idea. So did Strouse, who had written the music for a string of Broadway hits, including *Bye Bye Birdie* and *Applause*. But Charnin won them over. It took even more arm-twisting for him to get financial backing for the show; but finally, the production made it to East Haddam.

Now, with Andrea in the lead and some changes in the script, there was talk that the show might be headed for Broadway. In fact, Mike Nichols was so taken by the play that he called it a "gold mine" and joined up as a producer, along with his friend Lewis Allen. So the Broadway dream was more than just idle talk. Maybe I'd have another shot at it then, I thought. I could always dream, couldn't I?

A Lot of "Ifs"

My fantasies were reinforced by Martin Charnin, a casual guy who always struck up a friendly conversation about my broken arm every time I bumped into him. "When's the cast coming off?" he would say.

"In two weeks," I responded, knowing full well that it was going to be a lot longer. I figured that if he thought it was coming off soon, my dreams of being in the show might come true.

The truth is that Martin is just a nice guy who knows how to relate to kids because he has a daughter my age. He was probably just being friendly. But I interpreted his interest as a sign that he might want me to be in the show.

As the days went on, the dream of being in *Annie* loomed larger in my mind. When I finally went home to New Jersey, my head was spinning with thoughts of being on stage. But my only hope for a chance to be in *Annie* was for the show to go on Broadway and for some of the orphans to be bumped from the cast. A lot of "ifs" stood in the way of my dream, and all I could do was wait.

There's often a lot of waiting in show business—waiting for the results of an audition, waiting to say your few lines if you've got a minor part, or waiting for the big chance to play the featured role if you're an understudy. In the weeks after I left Andrea and the kids at the Goodspeed, I learned how to wait creatively.

Waiting in the Wings

I knew I couldn't just sit around until fall, hoping that *Annie* would be slated for Broadway and that there would be another open call. So I auditioned and won a part as an understudy for the role of Flora in a play called *The Innocents,* which had a brief run on Broadway.

The play had a star-studded cast, headed by Claire Bloom, and was directed by Harold Pinter. For six long weeks I was on the road, and for six long weeks I stood in the wings, waiting for a chance to go on stage.

Every day during the pre-Broadway run in Philadelphia and Boston, I spent hours in rehearsal. I was ready to go on at a moment's notice. But night after night, I just sat and watched my friend Sarah Jessica Parker perform the role. (Ironically, she later was *my* understudy in *Annie* and then succeeded me in the role!)

For some reason, even though every other understudy was given a chance to perform on stage at least once prior to Broadway, Harold Pinter never invited me to go on. Maybe it had something to do with that broken arm of mine.

I'm standing with "Big Daddy" Martin Charnin, who created and directed Annie, *at a cast party while I was appearing in the show as the orphan Kate. Near us is Kim Fedena, who took over the orphan role from me after I became Annie. Bill Yoscary*

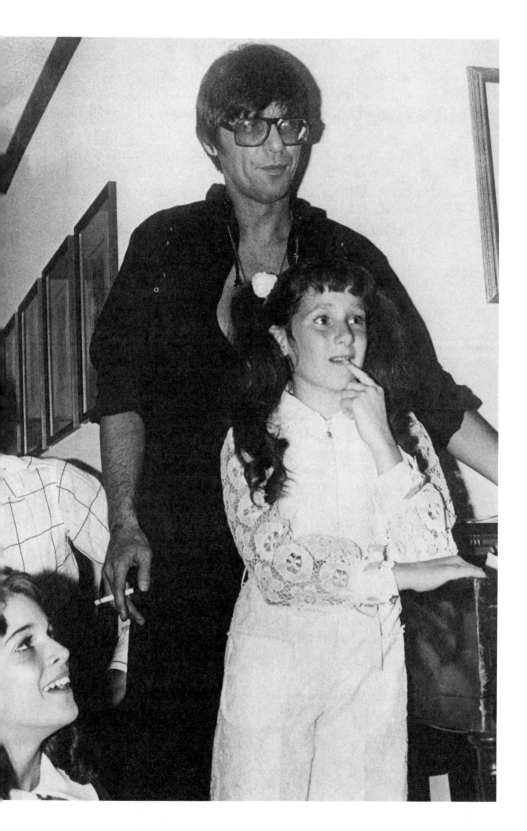

During the first day of rehearsal, I bumped into Pinter coming up the theater aisle. He took one look at my cast and said, "What did you do to your arm?"

"You hired me with a broken arm," I reminded him. During the audition for The Innocents I had worn a long-sleeved white blouse over the cast, so I guess he hadn't noticed. Well, he *had* noticed it when rehearsals started, so maybe that was the cause of my waiting game.

At any rate, I didn't have to wait much longer, because the play closed on Broadway a few weeks after it opened. In the long run, it didn't really matter that I was kept waiting in the wings, because the more I waited, the more I grew determined to get up on the stage of a major theater. The Innocents had given me a taste of Broadway, and I knew without a doubt it was where I wanted to be.

A Whole New Ballgame

A few weeks after the show closed, I picked up a copy of the trade paper Backstage and saw the announcement I had been waiting for: An open call for Annie was coming up soon. The show was headed for Broadway, and there were openings for three new orphans. For some reason, some of the girls who had played the roles at the Goodspeed had been dropped from the cast, and it was a whole new ballgame.

This time, I was ready. Martin Charnin was in the theater for the auditions, and although he remembered me from my visit to Connecticut, it certainly didn't mean I was a shoo-in. I went through three auditions, each one about three hours long.

When I made the "cut" (those chosen from the first audition), I was thrilled.

When I made it for the second, I was delirious.

By the time the phone call came through telling me I had the role of Kate, I was flying!

The euphoria didn't last long, however. Although I was a full-fledged member of the cast, I discovered it would be a couple of weeks before rehearsals would begin. The reason was money. The producers were having trouble raising the $250,000 they needed to get the show rolling. That meant we all had to sit tight and wait— and waiting was a skill I was developing into a fine art.

For some reason, the only people who seemed to have faith in the show were Charnin, Meehan, Strouse, and the producers. Finally, they gave the green light to go ahead, and rehearsals were set to begin. But on the very first day of rehearsal, the money still had not been raised and we waited at the rehearsal hall in vain as they told us to come back another day.

An eleventh-hour appeal by Mike Nichols and Lewis Allen to Roger Stevens of the Kennedy Center saved the day. Stevens and producer James Nederlander came through with the needed cash, and *Annie* was on its way. Rehearsals finally began on January 22, 1977, and, just three months later, we opened on Broadway.

A Pre-Broadway Run

Right from the start I felt at home with *Annie*. When I went in for the first rehearsal—which is just a basic reading of the script with everybody in the cast—I was already among friends. Andrea was there, of course, and I knew some of the other orphans from my visit to the Goodspeed and from the audition circuit. There was tiny Danielle Brisebois, seven, who played the youngest orphan, Molly; Robyn Finn, fourteen, as the oldest, wisest, and toughest orphan, Pepper; Janine Ruane, thirteen, as the blonde, glamourous orphan, July; Donna Graham, twelve, as Duffy; and Diana Barrows, eleven, as the nervous orphan, Tessie. At eleven, and as the second smallest in the group, I rounded out the cast of orphans in the role of Kate who was supposed to be seven and a little shy.

The adults in the cast were loaded with talent. I had seen Reid Shelton as Daddy Warbucks up in Connecticut and had fallen in love with his gruff, tough exterior and soft heart. A newcomer to the cast was Dorothy Loudon, who as Miss Hannigan, the director of The New York Municipal Orphanage in the play, knocked us all off our feet with her broad humor and socko singing. Last but not least, of course, was the fair-haired dog, Sandy, a real-life mutt who had been rescued from a pound in Connecticut moments before he was to be put to sleep.

From the moment we started rehearsals, the show was one exciting adventure after another. The most exciting of all was our five-week, pre-Broadway run at the Kennedy Center in Washington D.C., where we were feted at every turn.

Our first night in Washington, though, I wasn't sure I wanted to stick around for the fun. I hate bugs, and when I walked into the hotel room that was supposed to be my home for the next five weeks, I found myself surrounded by roaches. The next room they gave us was also overrun by the little creatures, and by the time we got to the last room, I wasn't anywhere in sight.

Here I am in my curly red wig just after tak-ing over the title role in Annie, *surrounded by the six orphans (clockwise, from top left): Kim Fedena, Donna Graham, Diana Barrows, Sarah Parker, Robyn Finn, and Danielle Brisebois.* Martha Swope

"Where's Michele?" my father asked, growing concerned because by then it was three o'clock in the morning. My parents found me sitting on top of my portable TV at the end of the hall, crying my eyes out.

Without a moment's delay, we moved into the Watergate, where we stayed until the end of the run. It was a wonderful place for a family to set up housekeeping—and that's exactly what we did. My mom stayed with me most of the time, and my dad would come down on weekends. Once, when my mom had to go home for a friend's funeral, my grandmother took her place and quickly got to work in our kitchenette making homemade spaghetti sauce. The aroma of her cooking wafted through the halls of the stately Watergate, and the minute I got off the elevator at our floor my nose told me that Grandma was at work, and I felt right at home. For a few moments, at least, I could leave the razzle-dazzle of show business behind.

Having the Run
of the White House

I never realized what it was like to be a star until we hit Washington. Even though I had the smallest speaking part among the orphans, it didn't matter to people in Washington. *Everybody* in the cast was a big celebrity as far as they were concerned. President Jimmy Carter thought so much of us that he invited the cast over to the White House on the night of our first preview at the Kennedy Center to give a command performance for the Governor's Ball.

But what made that evening so memorable—at least to us kids—wasn't our visit to the White House. It was what happened onstage earlier that night. We were right in the middle of a big scene at the orphanage, when all of a sudden Dorothy Loudon took a step and got her foot caught in the treadmill that was designed to take the actors across the stage in the New York City scene. We took one look at Dorothy and started screaming—and the curtain came down with a bang.

Luckily, Dorothy wasn't hurt, and we went off to the White House, ready to take on the President, the governors, and everyone else who was anybody. The orphans were such a hit that we were invited back a couple of times just to play with Amy Carter. The first time we went, we got all dressed up because somehow it didn't seem quite right to wear jeans to the White House. Amy, though, was more realistic. She greeted us at the door in a denim jumpsuit with a torn sleeve.

We practically had the run of the White House. I did cartwheels down the halls, bowled in the private bowling alley in the basement, and had milk and cookies that Mrs. Carter sent down. It was like being a real-life Annie in a real-life mansion! I had so much fun that day that I ruined a brand-new knit suit my mother had bought me for the occasion. When we left, we felt so at home that we said to Rosalynn Carter, "Say goodbye to Jimmy!"

The Secret Service practically became our bosom buddies because they were often at the theater escorting the high and the mighty. I couldn't believe that people like Henry Kissinger and Gerald Ford would actually be coming backstage to see me—but they did. And this was just the beginning.

We were considered such VIPs that for a while we had our own Secret Service escorts from the theater to our hotels. A few blocks from the show, some terrorists were holed up with some hostages they had snatched from the streets. The authorities had no idea what the terrorists would do next, and since *Annie* was so popular, we were considered possible targets. So an agent was assigned to each of us until the situation cooled off.

Praise and Partying

Our days were whirlwinds. We orphans lunched at Sans Souci, the fabulous watering hole of all the "in" people in Washington, where we were interviewed by a columnist from the *New York Daily News*. Andrea and I wore identical red and white checked gingham dresses our mothers had bought, but we parted company at the menu: She ordered côte de veau, while I played it safe with filet mignon. For drinks, we had a round of "Orphan Annies"—a combination of orange juice and grenadine that tastes like orange popsicles.

By the time the show got to Broadway, we had had so much praise and partying that it was almost a letdown. Personally, I was a little disappointed because my role was cut back as a result of last-minute changes in the script. All during the run in Washington, the play was being revised and perfected. The New York City scene, for example, where the cast moves across the stage on a big conveyor belt, had new stage directions almost nightly, causing massive confusion in the cast. Musical numbers were changed and added, lines in the script were cut, and characters were reshaped. As a result, the few lines I had when we opened at the Kennedy Center had been reduced to one line: "A dead mouse." I said it as I stuck a mouse in Miss Hannigan's face, scaring her half to death. I have to admit that I put everything I could into that one little line.

Rave Reviews

My disappointment at having such a small role was

I'm sitting pretty in the arms of Daddy Warbucks (Reid Shelton), but Sandy and Miss Hannigan (Alice Ghostley, the second actress to play the role) are unimpressed.
Jack Timmers

quickly forgotten as I got caught up in the madcap pace of being part of a smash hit. *Annie* opened at the Alvin Theatre on April 21, 1977, to fabulous reviews, and from then on we were all on "Easy Street."

Andrea was called a "pint-sized Liza Minnelli" who projected "pure pluck," and everyone fell in love with the orphans. What really tickled me was that Clive Barnes, the top *New York Times* theater critic, had singled me out as an "entrancing moppet." Even though I only had one line, I must have been doing something right! It was heady stuff for an eleven-year-old.

The reviews were such raves that the entire cast went crazy at the opening night party at Gallagher's Steak House. Sandy, the dog, was there all dressed up in a black bow tie, and I was dressed to the teeth in a green organza dress with a frilly pinafore apron. As the night wore on, Andrea and I got giddier and giddier, until finally we were mugging for our moms' cameras with a couple of balloons stuck up under our dresses to look like bustles.

Even after opening night, the excitement of *Annie* seemed to go on and on. The city was ours. Every paper and TV station in town wanted to interview us, and every charitable benefit wanted us to perform. Just after the show opened, the orphans were on the *Today Show*, where we were interviewed by Gene Shalit. All seven of us were up at the crack of dawn with our mothers and fathers by our sides, waiting to go on the show. We were so casual about the whole thing that while we waited to go on, we ended up playing jacks in the hall.

Every day was a new adventure. One afternoon, as a publicity stunt, we were issued full baseball uniforms—including jerseys emblazoned with a big "A" on the front—and took on the Bad News Bears in a softball game in Central Park. The boys were in town to promote their movie, *The Bad News Bears in Breaking Training*, and we gave them a run for their money. Even Governor Hugh Carey, who had a keen sense for a good photo opportunity, turned out to cheer us on. We lost, but we came out ahead with lots of photos in the New York City newspapers.

On our first day off after the show opened, we orphans joined the entire cast of *Annie* in a recording studio to make the original cast album. As I walked into the huge studio, which was a renovated Greek church in midtown Manhattan, my eyes bulged at the sight before me. Microphones and lights hung from the ceiling, and I had to pick my way across giant cables strewn all over the floor. But I really got goosebumps when someone told me that this was the same studio where Columbia had recorded *My Fair Lady* a quarter of a century earlier.

The recording took an entire day—from ten in the morning until midnight. But it wasn't as exhausting as it seemed because we worked in shifts. Union rules required that we be paid double if we worked longer than nine hours, so our songs were carefully scheduled in order that we could do all of our numbers and leave as quickly as possible.

After performing *Annie* on stage, it felt a little strange to belt out "It's the Hard Knock Life" and other orphan songs without an audience in front to applaud and cheer us on. It seemed even funnier to simply stand in front of a microphone in our jeans and sing, rather than jumping around in costume and adding broad gestures and facial expressions to put the songs across.

But somebody was listening very carefully to what we were singing. Every now and then a loudspeaker would crackle, and an anonymous voice from inside the sound booth would bark instructions, reminding us that even though we weren't on stage, this performance had to be *perfect*.

If there were any drawbacks to the stage life—what with performing in eight shows a week and squeezing in studying with tutors during the day—I never had time to think about them. I was too busy to notice that I rarely had time for friends outside of the show or that any semblance of a family life had disappeared. All of that would have to wait until tomorrow—because right now every minute was accounted for.

We got up on stage every day and made people laugh and cry, and we were automatically a success. After the show every night, people were lined up at the stage door to get a glimpse of us.

Backstage with Celebrities

Rarely a night went by when somebody famous wasn't in the audience. We kids even had a secret code worked out to help spot celebrities from the stage. Through a series of subtle coughs and gestures, we'd signal to each other to check out Section one, seat three, where one of our idols was sitting.

What's more, those celebrities I had yearned to meet all my life often actually came back stage after the show. Muhammad Ali came over to me, gave me a big hug, and dipped me back as though we were dancing in a Fred Astaire movie. Lee Majors and Farah Fawcett, who were then one of the hottest couples in show-business, came backstage and talked with us for a while; and even "the Fonz," Henry Winkler, stopped in the dressing room to trade stories. The day after Paul McCartney visited, he sent us swooning with gift boxes of Godiva chocolates that were delivered to our dressing room.

To a seventh-grader like me, it was the stuff dreams are made of. I had always thought celebrities would be kind of "standoffish," but they were as easy to talk to as

There were stars in my eyes backstage at the Alvin Theatre when Sammy Davis, Jr., dropped by to congratulate Dorothy Loudon (Miss Hannigan) and me on our performances in Annie. That night was my very first as an understudy in the title role, and I swooned when I spotted Davis in the audience. *Bill Yoscary*

the kid next door. Tony Orlando, for example, joined right into a conversation we were having about singers we liked. I said it had been one of my goals in life to meet Barbra Streisand someday because two of her films, *Hello, Dolly!* and *Funny Girl*, were my all-time favorites. When one of the girls whispered some negative report about Barbra that she had read in a gossip column, Tony set the record straight. "Don't believe that stuff," he said. "She's the nicest lady you'd ever want to meet."

Not long after, Barbra herself came backstage, and after I shook her hand and talked with her for a little while, I thought that now I had accomplished everything I had ever wanted in life! She was wearing a fur coat and Sandy kept barking at it, apparently waiting for a barking response. But, just as Tony Orlando had said, she was very down-to-earth and took all of the canine curiosity in stride.

Tony Award Time

As exciting as all these celebrity visits were, there was one star-studded event that left me positively breathless. I'm talking about the annual Antoinette Perry Awards, otherwise known at the "Tonys," Broadway's answer to the Oscars, which were presented in the Shubert Theater during a three-hour television spectacular on June 5, 1977.

All of the kids from *Annie* were scheduled to perform that night, and we were bubbling over with the excitement about the celebrities who would be in the audience. But to my surprise, the stars were out even for the rehearsals on the afternoon of the awards. My eyes were popping out of my head as I scanned the theater and saw the familiar faces of Tony Randall, Jack Albertson, Dionne Warwick, and Cleavon Little. *Everybody* was there, and it was overwhelming just to be with them.

Andrea, who had been nominated for Best Musical Actress, along with Dorothy Loudon, seemed a little more casual than the rest of us about the upcoming performance. Right after our rehearsal, she pulled out her skateboard and started riding it up and down Shubert Alley, the stretch of pavement right next to the Shubert Theater. When Martin Charnin heard about it, he was furious, and he ordered her not to skateboard until after the Tonys were over, just in case she broke a leg or an arm or something. Andrea wasn't thrilled at being told what to do, but for the sake of *Annie* and the awards that were at stake, she relented.

All of Broadway turned out for the awards ceremony, and the atmosphere in the theater was electric. We ran onstage in our raggedy orphans' costumes and pumped up the audience even more with a rousing rendition of "Smile"—an upbeat celebration of joy that ended with us shouting out, "Smile, darn ya, smile."

To thunderous applause, we rushed backstage to our dressing rooms to wait for the awards announcements. Every time *Annie* won an award, we screamed with delight, and by the time the awards ceremony was over, we were almost hoarse.

Annie had walked away with the Tonys, winning seven awards beginning with best musical. Dorothy Loudon had won for best musical actress, and although Andrea was disappointed, she didn't show it. The list of *Annie* winners went on and on: Thomas Meehan for best book, Charles Strouse and Martin Charnin for best score, David Mitchell for best scenic design, Peter Gennaro for best choreography, and Theonie Aldredge for best costume design.

Afterward, we kept the celebration going at the Hilton Hotel, where a big bash was planned for everyone from the Tonys. I wore a long blue velvet dress with a white lace pinafore that I had bought for the occasion, and I put my long hair up in pigtails. It was even more fantastic than I imagined, and my whole family showed up to rub shoulders with the stars and share in the excitement. My parents and grandparents were there, and what thrilled me even more was that my big brother Jimmy even came with a date!

Jimmy had always been one of my biggest fans, and when I first opened in *Annie,* he often bragged about me at the United Parcel Service office where he was working to put himself through Rutgers University. The funny thing was that the fellows at UPS didn't believe him, so he had to bring in a *Playbill* from *Annie* to prove that I was his sister.

I was so happy that *Annie* was something my whole family could enjoy together. While other families spent their free time cleaning the yard or sailing or going on outings, we spent ours at gala events like the Tony Awards! The only drawback to living a life like the stars was that it could sometimes be expensive. The "banquet" at the Hilton after the Tony's was fifty dollars-a-head, and all they served was eggs Benedict—with no seconds!

What made the expense and time worthwhile, though, was that the cast of *Annie* was the toast of the Tonys. During the party we were surrounded by stars who wanted to shake our hands and talk about the show. Even after the excitement of the Tonys died down, the accolades seemed to go on and on.

I'll have to admit that all this attention was overwhelming, and sometimes it went to our heads. After all, we were really just a bunch of ordinary kids who had been suddenly thrust into the limelight. Like any group of preteens, we responded by being giddy and silly and doing little practical jokes onstage, which we thought no one would notice.

Stage Business

One of the biggest pranksters was Annie herself, Andrea McArdle. Once, to break the monotony of doing the show day in and day out, she bought a jar of "slime"— a jellylike substance from the dime store. Right before an important scene where Annie is supposed to meet President Roosevelt's cabinet, Andrea coated her palm with the gooey stuff. Then she marched onstage, stuck out her hand, and greeted each of the cabinet members with a slimy handshake and a "How do you do?"

Those of us watching in the wings cracked up as we saw several slightly aghast actors try to keep their composure while deciding what to do with their hands.

During another performance, Andrea waited until the very end of the show to pull one of her jokes. With a bag of cotton balls in her hand just before the curtain call, she crept up behind actor Reid Shelton, who played Daddy Warbucks, and stuck some cotton balls on the back of his polyester suit.

The static electricity from the suit held the balls to his back until he bent over to take his bow. With thunderous applause ringing in his ears, Reid stepped forward and bowed deeply, only to be greeted by gales of laughter from the audience. The cotton balls had rolled off his back and were now stuck to the top of his sweaty, bald head. Reid was not amused.

But I suppose it could be said that Andrea got her just desserts a few weeks later, when she took a few hard knocks on stage. This time I was the unwitting culprit.

I was behind the curtain, waiting for a cue to run onstage. I had to pick up my bucket for the song, "It's a Hard Knock Life," which the orphans sing while they're cleaning up the orphanage at four a.m. As usual, I was concentrating on what I had to do next. I was supposed to run behind the row of iron beds onstage and pick up my pail, which was on the other side of the stage. The buckets had already been put in their appointed places by the stage hands, and I knew that Andrea would be picking hers up on my right as I ran in.

For some reason, though, Andrea's bucket had been placed on my left by mistake, and as I ran onstage, she was leaning over to pick hers up. I was running so close on her heels that I didn't have time to change direction. So I careened into her, sending her flying against the iron bed, where she knocked her head against the bedpost.

Before I even realized what had happened, she had passed out on the floor with a bloody nose. One of the girls gave her a slap on the back, and miraculously she bounced back up and finished the matinee—as well as half of the evening performance.

By then, though, it was clear something was wrong. It turned out that she had a concussion, and the doctor prescribed rest. But a day later she was up again, ready for a full schedule of performances.

Of course whenever Andrea was out sick, an understudy stepped into the role of Annie. For the first six months of our run, Kristin Vigard, who had played Annie when it had first opened at the Goodspeed Opera House, was Andrea's understudy. In August, though, three of us tried out for the understudy role, and I was chosen.

I'll have to admit that ever since I had started in the show, I had dreamed that someday I would be picked to play Annie. In a way, it was the unspoken dream of each of us orphans. But I was also very realistic about my prospects. When I started out, I knew that I was too young for the role. Still, I knew that the day would come when I'd be ready, and I hoped against hope that I'd be the lucky one.

It wasn't that I wanted to push Andrea out of the way.

It was just that Annie was such a joyful, upbeat role, and the songs were so much fun to sing. When I was alone at home or practicing with my voice coach, I'd belt out "Maybe," or "Tomorrow," and I'd get so caught up in the character that I felt like Annie. Those highs and lows of exhilaration and tears Annie felt were powerful stuff for me to experience, and I wanted more.

When I finally got my shot at the role as an understudy, I was confident that I was more than ready. After all, I had memorized the entire script not long after the show opened. I knew every line and every song by heart, and I could walk through Annie's paces with my eyes closed if I had to.

"The Hard Knock Life"

But when Andrea went on vacation to California for a week in September, leaving me with eight performances to do, I began to have grave doubts about whether I could do it. Up to then I had said only one line on stage. Even though that was well received, it wasn't exactly the same as saying *hundreds* of lines as Annie.

I tried to calm myself by thinking that the part was really no different from being an orphan, except that there were more lines. But it didn't work. I was scared stiff—for one solid week.

Even Sandy could sense my lack of confidence. The first night I got on stage, I stepped on his foot, and he took off like lightning. A few scenes later, I nearly fainted when I looked out in the audience and saw Sammy Davis, Jr., sitting in the third or fourth row. "Oh no, Sammy Davis!" I said to myself, overwhelmed that he was watching me perform. After the curtain came down, he rushed backstage to see me. In one of those tender, romantic gestures he's known for, he took my face in his hands, looked me deep in the eyes, and said, "You were *wonderful.*" I could have died.

But even the winsome words of a superstar like Sammy Davis couldn't reassure me. The second night, I forgot to sing the Annie line during "It's the Hard Knock Life." Instead, I sang along with the orphans. On the third night, I rattled Sandy so much that he pulled out of his collar and dashed across the stage.

By the time the week ended, I was running a 100-degree fever and was so desperate I called Andrea in California. "Can you come home?" I pleaded. "I can't take any more."

On the final day of my week as Annie, I was so sick I could barely move. My temperature had risen to 103, and I was so weak that during a scene when I was supposed to kick up my heels and run down some steps into Daddy Warbucks' arms, I tripped and fell, and Reid Shelton had to pick me up and carry me offstage.

The scene turned out to be so touching that the audience was sobbing. "Oh, she looks so pathetic," people whispered to one another.

I was pathetic, all right. I had had my big chance to play Annie, and I responded to the demand of a leading role by getting ill from exhaustion.

Could I ever make it on my own as Annie? As the final curtain came down, my mom and dad carried me off to our car and my cozy bed, where I slept like a baby.

At the Top

There *is* no business like show business—take it from me.

After my week's run as Annie, I was sitting morosely in my living room at home, recuperating from my illness, when the front door bell rang. "Delivery for Shelley Bruce," said the voice outside.

I opened the door and the messenger handed me a tiny robin's-egg-blue package from Tiffany's, wrapped in red ribbon. I gave a little start, because the package was done up exactly like the one that Daddy Warbucks gives Annie in the show, with a silver locket inside.

The attached note was written in the same color blue ink as the package.

"Dear Shelley," it read. "I was in Tiffany's today and picked this thing up for you. It's to commemorate that lovely performance when real tears flowed, and it was so real you made me cry.

"Thank you, my dear little one, for being such a pro when you weren't feeling well. Love, Reid.

"P.S. I came here to get a silver locket and would you believe they don't have *any!*"

I wept as I read the note, remembering a tender moment between Reid and me the week before during the scene when Annie learns that Daddy Warbucks is going to adopt her. Daddy Warbucks had looked me in the eyes and said, "I love you, Annie," and at that moment, I had felt as if I *were* Annie. With tears streaming down my face, I had answered, "I love you, too."

Carefully, I opened the box. Inside was a tiny blue pouch holding a single silver teardrop on a silver chain.

Reid Shelton's gift was the medicine I needed. There had been some wonderful moments during that week as Annie, and even though I ended up sick as a dog, I had "carried on" and given it my best shot.

What more could anyone have done? I asked myself.

That question was laid to rest a few days later when I received a touching letter from Dorothy Loudon, whom I had grown to love dearly during our months on stage together. Her words went right to the heart of what I was feeling. "What a letdown it must be for you to have been Annie for a week and then suddenly not be Annie, just as you were getting your teeth into it," she wrote. "You are a trouper in the true sense of the word. And I am proud to have been on stage with you. There will be many wonderful parts ahead just waiting for you. I love you."

Dorothy knew what she was talking about. She had been through the ups and downs of the theater many times herself. I was touched that even now, in the midst of deep personal tragedy following the death of her husband, she had found the time to reach out and encourage *me* to look to tomorrow.

Now it was up to me to bounce back and play my little role as Kate with all I had in me and be ready to bowl over the crowds as Annie whenever Andrea was unable to do the show. That's what a pro like Reid or Dorothy would do. So, that's what I resolved to do, too.

Fitting the Part

During the next few months, I stepped in for Andrea nineteen times, and before long the role was beginning to fit like a kid glove. I loved playing Annie, and I wanted the experience to go on and on. Reporters often asked me if I hoped that Andrea would get sick so that I could go on stage—but I was too much of a professional to even think of such a thing. I knew, though, that the time would be coming soon when she would step down from the role and move on to other things. Her one-year contract would be up in March 1978, and soon it became clear that she would not be continuing for another year.

At fourteen, Andrea was "too old" to play eleven-year-old Annie. Already, some of the orphans had out-grown their roles and been replaced by younger, smaller girls, and now it was Andrea's turn. She would be doing the show in London for a couple of months, and after that she'd put Annie behind her and start life as an adult actress. The big question in everyone's mind, especially mine, was, Who will replace her?

After weeks of wondering, I got the official word from Peter Neufeld, the general manager of the show, that I was under consideration. "I'll get back to you in two weeks with the decision," he told me.

For those two weeks, I was in agony. I was used to waiting for the results of auditions, and it had never both-ered me before. But this time was different. I had given a year of my life to the show, and I knew how exciting it was to play Annie. So I knew how much I had to lose.

Two weeks passed, and I didn't hear a word from Neufeld. I let a few more days go by, and still there was no call or letter telling me the results.

Finally, I couldn't take it anymore. I picked up the phone, called Neufeld, and said, "I've just *gotta* know. *Please* tell me."

"The part is yours," he said.

The minute I heard his words, I burst into tears.

"No, no, no—you don't understand," he said. But I was so choked up I couldn't even voice a response, and I handed the phone to my mother.

"Shelley doesn't understand," Neufeld told her. "She's got the part."

"Yes," said my mom, "she understands. That's why she's crying. She's so happy."

Leapin' Lizards, I was Annie!

How can I explain the sheer thrill of becoming the curly-haired redhead who was America's darling. Annie was more than just a part in a play. She was a tradition of optimism, spunk, and clean-cut morality who had captured the heart of America from the moment Harold Gray's comic strip *Little Orphan Annie* hit the pages of the *New York Daily News* in 1924. For more than half a century, *everybody* has loved Orphan Annie, the homeless waif who suffered through trials and tribulations with her dog Sandy and found happiness under the wing of her foster father, the archconservative billionaire, Daddy Warbucks.

The Plot Line

When Annie hit Broadway, she established a brand-new tradition that embellished the original and tugged even harder at the emotions of a country wracked by Vietnam and Watergate and hungering for happier times. As a matter of fact, the only link between the new Annie and the old were the characters of Annie, Warbucks, and Sandy, which were taken from the comic strip. After that, the Broadway Annie was her own person—with a background and story created from the ground up by writer Thomas Meehan.

As Broadway's Annie, I started out life in an orphanage, where I had been left on the steps as a baby by my parents, who were too poor to care for me. Despite the drill-sergeant tactics of the orphanage director, Miss Hannigan, I managed to keep up my spirits during my eleven years of life, and I dreamed that someday my parents would turn up to save me from the dreary life I was leading. But I was also a realist, and in my pocket was tangible proof of my hope: half of a locket, left behind by my parents, and a note from them that said: "We've kept the other half, so that when we come back for her, you'll know she is our baby."

As I waited for my parents' return, my main mission in life at the orphanage was to look after the other girls and boost their spirits by standing up to our nemesis— Miss Hannigan.

Once, during an escape attempt from the orphanage, I found a stray dog, whom I named "Sandy." A policeman finally caught me and Sandy with a bunch of bums in a shantytown called "Hooverville." Sandy escaped, but the policeman marched me back to the orphanage. Fortunately, I didn't have to stay there long. A lovely lady named Miss Farrell, who was the private secretary to a very rich man named Oliver Warbucks, came to the orphanage and chose me to spend a week at his mansion for Christmas.

Little by little I wormed my way into the heart of the

gruff Oliver Warbucks, who soon wanted me to become his little girl. One special evening, he handed me a little blue box from Tiffany's, which held a brand-new locket to replace my broken one. As much as I loved "Daddy" Warbucks, though, I wanted more than anything in the world to be reunited with my own parents. So, Daddy Warbucks swallowed his disappointment and waged a one-man campaign to find them, offering a $50,000 reward to the couple who could prove they were my parents.

In the meantime, Miss Hannigan's brother, Rooster, a wily ex-con, got wind of the offer, and he and his girlfriend, Lily, decided to pose as my parents. Miss Hannigan got caught up in the scheme when she gave them the other half of my locket from a dusty file. Unbeknownst to me, my parents were dead, and I was all alone in the world.

While the search for my parents continued, Daddy Warbucks took me to Washington, D.C., to meet President and Mrs. Roosevelt. I gave the President's cabinet a peptalk on positive thinking and even helped usher in the New Deal with the song "Tomorrow."

Back in New York, hundreds of couples were waiting outside Daddy Warbucks mansion, claiming to be my parents. They all proved to be fakes, and so Daddy Warbucks planned a special Christmas Eve party to sign the papers to adopt me.

But just as he was about to sign the papers, in walked Rooster and Lily with the other half of my locket. Rooster's ruse nearly worked, and Daddy Warbucks told him to come back on Christmas to get me—and the

---

Sandy and me, at age twelve, when I took over the role as Annie. Martha Swope

reward money. But Miss Farrell grew suspicious, and so Daddy Warbucks enlisted President Roosevelt and the FBI to put a trace on Rooster's alias and check the hand-writing on the note from my parents. The report came back that Rooster was a fraud and that my parents were dead.

When Rooster and Lily came to get me on Christmas day, the cops were waiting to take them and Miss Hannigan to jail.

My story ended with the most wonderful Christmas party in the world, where, surrounded by my orphan friends and my own Daddy Warbucks, I looked forward to a life filled with sunny tomorrows.

That was my new life as Annie, and I lived that role six days a week—twice on Wednesdays and Satur-days—for one glorious year, beginning on February 28, 1978.

Just before I took over the role, I had my first vacation since joining the cast of Annie. My parents and I spent a wonderful week together in Puerto Rico, lounging on the beach and seeing the sights in San Juan. But, in truth, the vacation wasn't all pleasure. My dad spent a lot of time on the phone to New York negotiating my contract, and up until a few days before I was to step into the role, we still hadn't nailed everything down. The big problem for me was that they wanted to give me a "four-week-out." That meant that every four weeks I'd either be in the show or out of it.

Somehow that arrangement didn't seem fair, and even though it was only three months before my twelfth birth-day, I was old enough to know what I wanted. I didn't want to be on a yo-yo, wondering about my future every month. I wanted job security and the chance to grow in the part, at least for a year. Finally, that's what I got, and I flew back to New York ready to become Annie.

Looking and Acting the Part

Although I knew the role cold because of my stints as understudy, there were a few adjustments I had to make to step into Annie's shoes. In the first place, I had to look like Annie, and that meant that my long brown hair, which reached below my waist, had to be cut off. Just so I wouldn't get upset, the hairdresser cut it off in two different sittings a few days before the opening. The first time, he cut it to my waist; the second time, he cut it shoulder-length and dyed it red.

Secondly, I had to win over one member of the cast whose relationship to me on stage was critical: Sandy. After Andrea left, Sandy was traumatized. He moped around the theater for days, refusing to eat or play. He had worked with her ever since the show opened at the Goodspeed Opera House. On stage, Sandy and Annie were a team, and now it was up to me to make the teamwork a success.

Although he had gotten to know me from the times I had understudied for Andrea, it was important that the transition go perfectly. So, before the opening, Sandy and I spent time alone together with his owner and trainer, Bill Berloni, going over our "lines." Whenever Sandy performed on cue, I'd reward him with dog biscuits and a big hug. Since I had a poodle of my own named "Jacques" and I'm crazy about dogs, I knew that the most important thing for me to communicate to Sandy was how much I loved him. I was also very firm with him on and off stage, and that seemed to work as he quickly started to follow my commands. Little by little, Sandy began to trust me and respond like an old friend, and from then on, I only had to spend a few minutes before each show warming up with him.

The final step to being Annie was a "replacement

rehearsal" with the whole cast just before showtime, to be certain I had the lines and quick changes down pat. The tightest change came in the second act, when I had to switch in a matter of seconds from a sailor suit to the red Annie dress and curly wig. The way I did it was to start undressing as I walked offstage, peeling off my blouse and skirt as I moved out of the audience's line of sight. Just beyond the curtain stood a dresser, who waited with my red dress and Mary Jane shoes, and a hair-dresser, who held my wig. As soon as the dresser threw my dress over my head, the hairdresser pinned my hair up, put a stocking cap over it with a couple of pins, and then put the wig in place. Moments later, I ran back onstage, looking like the Annie of the comic strip.

The rehearsal went like clockwork, and a few hours later I was ready to become Annie.

Showtime!

That night, the minute I walked in my dressing room, I knew what it meant to be a star. I actually had not one but *two* dressing rooms: one for me and one for my mom, my poodle, and my costumes. Both of the rooms were so crammed full of flowers from well-wishers, I could barely sit down. There was even one arrangement that spelled out Annie in big styrofoam letters with little Annie dolls sticking out every which way. It was from my big brother Jimmy, and it made me smile to think he had taken special pains to make his gift different from the rest.

On my dressing table was a pile of telegrams cheering me on in my new role, and every now and then someone would run down to my mail slot by the stage door and pick up a few more that had come in.

Every so often, in the background, the room crackled with the sound of the intercom and the voice of the stage manager giving the countdown until showtime: "Half hour . . . fifteen minutes . . . five minutes."

Then, finally came the moment I had been waiting for: "Places," said the voice over the loudspeaker." I ran downstairs and took my place on an iron bed in the middle of the orphanage.

Once I went up on that stage, I never came down. I was on a high, spinning in a world called *Annie,* and I couldn't have gotten off, even if I had wanted to.

Critical Acclaim

The most exhilarating part of it all was the reviews. Fortunately, I didn't have to sit up all night on opening night sweating out the critics' reaction to my performance. Because I was taking over the role, the reviews appeared one by one over the next few months. As each one came in, I grew more and more confident of myself as an actress.

New York magazine's tough theater critic, John Simon, said my characterization of Annie was "more layered: This Annie is more devious and determined, more guarded and old before her time, and thus also in the last analysis, more touching." The *Chicago Tribune's* Aaron Gold wrote he was "moved to tears." "Miss Bruce has . . . warmth, charm and believability . . . " The show business trade paper, *Variety,* said: "Shelley Bruce . . . shows the proper waifish vulnerability and delivers her comedy lines with expert timing. She puts over the principal song, 'Tomorrow,' with full effectiveness."

That was *me* they were talking about! A few years before, such acclaim might have seemed unbelievable. But after a few months as Annie, I knew what it was like to be at the top and to be praised and fussed over like a princess. There was never a moment when I wasn't in demand. There were interviews to do—more than I had ever thought possible—along with ribbon cuttings, benefit performances, and TV appearances. *Everybody* wanted Annie. My fame spread even more when my picture was plastered across the pages of dozens of national magazines—including *Playboy*—in an ad for RCA Color Track TV. The only thing that kept me from being *too* overworked was the fact that I had to clear every interview or appearance with the Society for Prevention of Cruelty to Children to make sure I wasn't being "exploited!"

Star Billing—the Bad Side

I loved every minute of it, but I also learned quickly that despite all the attention I was getting, it was often lonely being a celebrity. The dark side of my new status as Annie was that I couldn't share my moments of triumph with anyone but my mom, my dog, and a few close friends in the show.

When I was an orphan, I had shared a dressing room with all the other kids, and we had loads of fun trading stories about the performance and sharing silly secrets. We even took turns running a snack bar together backstage, selling soda and cookies to the cast and crew. Between shows on matinee days, we used to get a big kick out of hanging out at a pinball room on Broadway. Steve, the owner, would let us work at the candy counter until showtime.

But now that I had my own dressing room across the stage from the rest of the kids, there was no time for things like snack bars; and most of the other girls kept their distance.

What's more, there were times when I sensed the resentment and jealousy of the other girls. Some of them even went so far as to carry the competition on stage. Kids who weren't supposed to wear makeup onstage would put it on anyway, in order to stand out. Others would fix their hair up when it was supposed to be messy. These were just silly little-girl antics that all pre-teen girls go through, and I tried to chalk it up to their age. But it hurt anyway.

I also learned fast that being a star was more than just fun and games and seeing my picture plastered all over the pages of national magazines. It was *hard work*, and it took an enormous amount of personal discipline and energy to keep up with it.

My first brush with reality came during my first week in the role. Right off the bat, the director laid down the law: There would be no fooling around by anyone—and that meant us kids. Unfortunately, although I had rarely been the instigator of any pranks in the past, I bore the brunt of the new regime of strictness because I was now the star. After every show I'd get notes on the performance, and if I so much as had my legs crossed the wrong way, I'd be scolded. But I swallowed my pride and decided that if this is what it took to be a professional, I'd *be* professional and show everybody just how tough I was.

If being a star meant taking your licks even when you didn't deserve them, it also meant being reliable—to the minute. A theatrical contract is like a marriage vow. When the curtain went up, I had to be at the theater, for better for worse, in sickness and in health, until my contract ran out.

As with any job, there were some days when I just didn't feel like going to work. I'd rant and rave around the house and say to my mother, "I am not going in today—I'm *not* going in." But, five minutes later, I'd be dressed and ready to hop in the car for the ride to Manhattan. I simply didn't have a choice in the matter. Even though I was only thirteen, I had a job, I was under contract, and I had to go in. Even the television and charity appearances were part of the package I had signed up for when I agreed to be Annie. It was all part of show business, and I accepted it as a matter of course.

The Routine

My days were pretty much mapped out for me. I'd wake up about one or two in the afternoon, have a tutor from three until five, and at six o'clock my mother and I would leave for the show.

Usually, before the show, I'd stop by my vocal coach, Sue Seaton, to warm up. I'd sign in to the theater at seven-thirty and then yell to Jack, the production stage manager, "You'll know where I'll be." Then I'd walk down the block to Gallagher's, where in five minutes, my prime ribs—medium to rare—were on the table in front of me. The maître d' knew I had to do the show, and so he was always ready for me when I walked in the door. I had the same thing for dinner every night.

After the show, I wouldn't get home until midnight, but my father was often waiting for me with a chicken cooking in the oven. After performing for three hours straight, I was so wound up there was no way I could go to sleep the minute I got home. So I'd stay up until two and then fall asleep until the next afternoon. On matinee days, Wednesdays and Saturdays, my sleep would get cut short by a few hours, but I'd catch up on Mondays when the theater was "dark."

Not on the Program

Most of the time, the routine worked pretty well, and I

made it to the show a half hour before the curtain went up without a hitch. But one afternoon, I found myself stuck in traffic at Tenth Avenue and Fifty-second Street—two long city blocks from the theater—at exactly five minutes before the two o'clock matinee. I knew that if I sat in the car with my mother and brother, there was no way I was going to get to the matineee on time. I also realized that if I ran the two blocks, I'd be out of breath and too tired out to do my best on stage. So, I did the next best thing: I jumped on my brother's back and he carried me all the way to the theater. We made it by two, up went the curtain five minutes later, and on went the show.

Even when things went smoothly before showtime, there was never any guarantee that the show itself would go smoothly. Inevitably, someone would drop a line or a prop would be out of place, and I'd have to respond as though nothing had happened—always reacting as Annie would.

The worst thing of all, of course, was to be stuck on stage with no reaction at all. And that's exactly what happened in the middle of a serious scene where Daddy Warbucks and I discover that all the people claiming to be my parents were fakes.

I was sitting on a loveseat listening to Daddy Warbucks tell me how much he cared for me, when, all of a sudden, he turned to the audience and said, "Excuse me." With that, he walked off the stage.

I couldn't imagine what was happening, and for a few interminable seconds, I just sat there doing nothing, wondering what I should do. I kept my head down, almost laughing with nervousness because I didn't know what was going on. Then I heard Reid's voice, offstage—and so did everyone else in the theater.

"Will you be quiet, please!" he yelled at the stagehands.

Then, he walked onstage and went back into the part as if nothing had happened.

Most of the time, though, when mishaps occurred in the middle of a scene, I managed to recover and keep in character—even if I was in pain. One recurrent problem I had was a trick knee that kept bothering me when Daddy Warbucks and I danced the Peabody. We'd be facing each other, and I'd walk back four steps, pivot, and walk forward four steps. But whenever I'd pivot, inevitably my foot would stay planted on the floor, and I'd throw my knee out of joint.

In order to keep the image of Annie intact, somehow I struggled to make it through the scene without limping. Luckily, help was just offstage in the form of Bob Fitch, the tall and suave actor who played Rooster. I soon learned he could fix *anything*, and that included knowing exactly how to put pressure on my knee to make the pain go away. After a fix by Fitch, I'd run back on for the next scene.

In addition to his know-how with my knee, Bob fascinated us kids with the magic tricks he performed backstage to keep us from getting bored. And his sleight-of-hand also came in handy when he was conspiring with Miss Hannigan to get Oliver Warbucks' money and get rid of Annie. Brandishing an open switchblade, Fitch said, "When I want something to disappear, it disappears . . . " With that, the switchblade vanished from sight—as Rooster flashed a sinister smile and said, " . . . for good."

So Bob's "magic" certainly came in handy in keeping my leg in shape, but there were other problems I had to handle on my own. Once, right before the scene where Daddy Warbucks takes me into his office and gives me the locket from Tiffany's, I watched in anguish as the treadmill that moved the scenery broke the leg on the chair on which I was supposed to sit. Reid Shelton had his back turned at the time and didn't realize the chair had been broken.

I walked onstage, and he said, "Annie, sit down."

I didn't know what to do. I knew I couldn't sit on the chair, and so I tried to think of something that would clue him into the situation and keep the scene moving along. Without missing a beat, I said, "Miss Farrell said the chair is broken and the man hasn't come to fix it yet."

With that, he took another chair from the back of his desk and moved it to the side so I could sit down.

After weathering a crisis like that, it was always exciting for me, after the final curtain came down, to listen to the thunderous applause of the audience and know that they were none the wiser.

Lessons Learned

What all of these experiences added up to was that in my year as Annie I grew up—fast—as an actress and as a person. During that time I learned that I could handle myself with ease in any situation. I discovered that I could smile at a crowd when I felt like crying or show up for a grueling telethon when I felt like sleeping. Most of all, I knew that if I could perform eight shows a week, fifty-two weeks a year, I could discipline myself to do anything I wanted in life—anything.

But perhaps the most important lesson I learned as Annie came not from the discipline of the stage but from the example of a little five-year-old girl named Diana Garcia, who is the cerebral palsy poster child.

One of my many jobs as Annie was to appear at benefits and telethons, and the cerebral palsy telethon in 1979 promised to be one more stop in a very busy schedule. The telethon had started at the Ed Sullivan Theater on

Broadway at ten o'clock one Saturday morning, and the following day, prior to our Sunday matinee, I was on the TV show along with the other orphans.

My role was to sing "Tomorrow," and after I finished the song, the telethon hosts, Dennis James and Suzanne Somers, asked me to introduce the others. As I called their names, the girls stepped forward, one by one, and gave a little background on their characters. After introducing the six actresses, I turned to Dennis James, expecting him to thank us and move on to the next guests.

But instead, he looked at me and said, "Shelley, you *forgot* an orphan."

My face turned red, and I started to stammer a reply, when all of a sudden, across the floor, I spotted a darling little girl with blonde hair walking toward me on braces. She was walking very, very slowly, and with each step the tremendous effort she was exerting became more and more apparent.

Right before our eyes, Diana Garcia, the cerebral palsy poster child, was walking without crutches for the first time. Tears started welling up in my eyes as I watched her move across the stage, and before long she was standing next to me as Suzanne Somers steadied her.

"Diana," said Dennis James, "This year you've walked unassisted for the very first time. Maybe next year you'll start singing 'Tomorrow.' "

The words had scarcely left his lips when Diana, in a sweet, small voice, began to sing, "The sun will come out,

---

Sandy and I took a shortcut to signing autographs at a suburban mall at Christmas: We gave away photo copies of our pictures inscribed with his pawprint and my signature! Robert B. Wolin

tomorrow . . . " As she sang, something stirred deep within me, and before I knew it, I was singing along with her, "Bet your bottom dollar that tomorrow, there'll be sun . . . " Gradually, the band eased its way in, and before long our duet filled the studio.

Suddenly, in the background, the telephones started ringing off their hooks. The more we sang, the more the phones rang. It was one of those moments—unplanned and unabashedly emotional—that could never be duplicated, and for the next few hours, until the end of the telethon, the segment was replayed again and again.

Reluctantly, I left the studio to do a performance of *Annie*, but as soon as the show was over, I raced back to the telethon and stayed until it was over at seven P.M. Afterward, I spent a long time talking with Diana and her parents, Pat and Pete, and I was deeply touched by the little girl's strength and positive spirit. She told me very matter-of-factly that even though her future was uncertain, she was determined to get better. What affected me even more was the simple, loving way she was willing to put her faith and physical struggle on the line before millions of people if it could help someone else.

In the months and years following the telethon, Diana and I became fast friends. Not long after we met, she went through an operation on her legs, and I visited her in the hospital. By the time the next cerebral palsy telethon came around in 1980, we had become so close that Diana and her family spent the night before the show at my house in New Jersey. During the telethon we sang duets of "You Light Up My Life" and "Tomorrow." The following year, when I was in the hospital, the whole Gar-

In my off-hours as Annie, I sang at dozens of events like this award ceremony for the Cartoonists' Society of America. Buck Peters

One of my most unforgettable experiences during my year as Annie was at this cerebral palsy telethon. Just moments before this photo was taken, Diana Garcia (center), a young cerebral palsy poster child, had walked without crutches for the first time in her life. As telethon hosts Suzanne Somers and Dennis James looked on, Diana and I broke into a chorus of "Tomorrow."

cia family came to visit me. Although Diana and her little sister, Jenna, had to wait in the lobby because they were too young to be permitted on the floor, I gained extra strength just knowing they were there. Today, Diana walks on her own without crutches or braces, and, inspired by her duets with Annie on the telethons, she is even taking singing lessons!

From the time we met on that first telethon, I sensed that something very special had come into my life. What drew me to Diana was her tremendous courage. In those few moments on the telethon, as I watched her walk painfully across the stage and joined with her to sing "Tomorrow," we shared an almost mystical communion. Somewhere, somehow, there was a message there for me.

But at the time I didn't understand why that experience on the telethon had moved me as it did. What's more, I couldn't imagine how Diana's courage in the face of severe illness had any relationship to me personally. I was a Broadway star, in the peak of health and success, and my biggest concern was how I was going to pull myself away from my theater family and say goodbye to my glorious year as Annie.

PART TWO

Photo by Jack Timmers

What Do I Do for an Encore?

Annie's creator, Martin Charnin, liked to joke that the minute one of us kids developed a waist and other appropriate feminine curves, the show was in trouble.

I guess my costumes must have hinted at a waist, because when my contract ran out in March 1979, so did my life as Annie. A few months before, Martin had taken my mom aside backstage and told her I was getting too big for the part. Then one day when we were alone together in my dressing room, she broke the news to me.

I had known all along that this part of my life would have to come to an end, and so I wasn't upset at all. Instead, oddly enough, I felt a strange kind of happiness because I felt so lucky to have had a whole year in the title role.

Closing the Door on Childhood

But as the day of my departure drew closer and closer,

the tears started to come. I felt like I was leaving part of my family behind, because, in a sense, that's what the cast and crew of a show like *Annie* are. I had lived with these people day in and day out in a highly charged emotional setting for two of my thirteen years of life.

What's more, I sensed that with the end of *Annie* I would also be closing the door on my childhood. Ahead of me was the adult world and a whole new realm of experiences and opportunities. Slowly, I began to realize that no matter how successful I was as a child star in *Annie*, I'd have to begin anew to build up my credentials and prove myself. In a very real sense, I would have to start all over again.

But I brushed aside the thoughts about my future as I tried to squeeze every last ounce of excitement out of my last few days as Annie. I focused instead on bidding goodbye to the people in the cast I had come to love.

The Gypsy Robe

The most difficult time of all wasn't my last performance but at a party the cast and crew gave me at Sardi's the Friday before I left the show. It was an intimate group—if you can call a gathering of a hundred people intimate. But everyone there was part of my theater family—either a member of the cast, crew, or production staff. They had all chipped in to buy two diamond eyes for a silver Annie head that had been given to me when I was an orphan. Along with the diamonds—as they said, "just so you won't forget us," as if I could—they presented me with a treasure that meant more to me than any gift money could buy.

It was a "gypsy robe"—a beige kimono bordered in green with signatures and mementos from everyone who had worked with me on *Annie*. Emblazoned on the back was my name, written in green calligraphy. In tiny letters was a message: "This robe was designed and executed with love and care for Shelley Bruce by Jane Robertson to commemorate her departure from the show *Annie* on March 4, 1979, after being with it for over two years. We'll miss you."

Under normal circumstances, a gypsy robe is passed from show to show and embellished with fabulous designs and memorabilia. One member of the cast will guard the robe until the show closes, and then it's passed on to another show, for new adornments and new memories. Although the shows may have died, each gypsy robe lives on as a reminder of the link among all theater people and of the dazzling life of show business.

What made my gypsy robe special was that it was mine—to keep forever. Jane Robertson, who had understudied for all of the adult female roles, had labored to put the robe together. Then, everyone who had shared *Annie's* fortunes with me had added notes and pictures to it. Reid Shelton had written his name in black laundry marker and had drawn a sketch of Daddy Warbucks' ears, bald head, and lapel. Stuck in the lapel was a sparkly rhinestone. Alice Ghostly, who had taken over Miss Hannigan's role after Dorothy Loudon left, drew a yellow whistle with little black notes coming out. Sandy and his understudy, a dog named "O'Malley," had even left their pawprints.

Everyone who had anything to do with the show had signed it—even New York's Mayor Ed Koch. I had seen the Mayor so often at the theater, Gracie Mansion, or charity benefits that I felt like he was practically a member of the cast. On the robe, he drew lots of faces with funny-shaped noses—the faces were all outlined in black, the noses in different colors.

Each drawing or poem brought back memories of my year as Annie. There was a picture of a Christmas tree with a banister behind it. At the top of the banister was me, and sliding down was Edie Cowen, who played Daddy Warbucks' maid. Coming out of her mouth in comic-book style was the saying, "Let's do it again sometime."

As I looked at Edie's cartoon, I remembered the day the cast paid a visit to Gracie Mansion, where we performed a skit for Mayor Koch. During a tour of the mansion, Edie and I lagged behind the others and found ourselves at the top of a long staircase with a newly polished banister. Edie looked at me, and I looked at her, and I said, "Let's do it." With that, we each took turns sliding down the banister. We never told anyone about the fun we had that day, and even the gypsy robe didn't give away our little secret.

Every fold of the robe held a message from someone special—the dressers, the lighting men, and the stage managers. On one sleeve was a big heart inscribed, "Jack Timmers loves Shelley" from our production stage manager. I smiled when I saw it, remembering how he liked to let off steam by playing the pinball machine I kept in my dressing room. On the front of the robe by the pocket was a beautiful unicorn surrounded by flowers. Chris Jamison, who played the role of the "Star to Be," had thoughtfully remembered how much I loved those mythical beasts.

The most cryptic message came from the bouncer for

One of my first appearances with New York City's Mayor Ed Koch was with Sandy at the Inner Circle—a society of press pundits known for "roasting" politicians. On stage, Mayor Koch played Daddy Warbucks as we sang "I Don't Need Anything But You," a duet from **Annie.** *Official City Hall Photograph by Holland Wemple*

the Alvin Theatre, George Roberson, a giant of a man whom we called "Big George." He was six foot six and was best known for the "killer cherries" that he soaked in liquor for six months. Big George later went on to bigger things as a bodyguard for Raquel Welch when she starred in *Woman of the Year.* But at the Alvin he was always on hand to kick out troublemakers in the theater. His note on my gypsy robe consisted of three red cherries.

The robe's most poignant memento of all, though, was a note written on a piece of brown paper bag and stuck in the pocket: "Please take care of our little girl," the note said. "Her name is 'Annie,' and she was born on October 28, 1922. We'll be back to get her soon." It was the same note that as Annie I had pulled out of my raggedy orphan's pocket night after night in the show, and already I could feel myself getting overcome with nostalgia.

But I brightened as I read the words our stage manager, Patrick O'Leary, had written on the robe: "Although you take your flight/Remember this night/So there will never be sorrows/In your tomorrows."

This *was* a night to remember—and a year to remember. As I clutched the gypsy robe in my arms, I knew my life would be shaped by *Annie* forever. What I didn't realize at the time was just how much I would draw on Annie's gritty example and my experience in the theater to get through an even more demanding role ahead.

The Final Curtain

I played my last show to a standing-room-only crowd that applauded and cheered at the end of each song I sang. Maybe that's because I had packed the audience with my friends and relatives! Whatever the reason, there was an electricity in the theater that night that made the evening feel more like opening night. But it was the end of an era—for me and for *Annie*—because I was the last of the original orphans to still be in the cast. The final curtain went down, and a silver limousine whisked me off to another goodbye bash thrown by my old friend Dick Miller for my family and friends.

But when the party was finally over and I said my goodnights, my glamourous life suddenly disappeared before my eyes. I stood in an empty parking lot feeling a little bit like Cinderella at midnight. The applause of the adoring crowds had died out, my silver limousine was gone, and in their place stood my parents and their little car, waiting to take me home to New Jersey.

Overnight I was transformed from a "star" into a "normal" suburban kid. My life suddenly became filled with a busy teenage routine of junior high, cheerleading, and talking on the phone with friends—things I had missed during my two years on Broadway.

But I found out fast that my life would never be really normal. No matter how much I tried to conform, there was a part of me that was different from the other kids because I had already had a taste of adult responsibility. Most kids don't have a chance to have real responsibility until they learn to drive or get a part-time job or start college. But being on stage makes you grow up fast; and at thirteen, I already knew how to operate effectively in the adult world.

Back on the Boards

In fact, I had never really left that world. A few months after leaving *Annie*, I was back on the boards in another Milliken industrial show, and by the fall of 1979 I was at the Goodspeed Opera House in a musical called *A Long Way to Boston*. It was the story of a mother, played

To give myself a new post-Annie look at age fourteen, I let my hair grow back to its natural brown. My hair, which once reached below my waist, was cut short and dyed red for the Annie role.

by Nancy Dussault, who goes out for the Boston Marathon, and I was one of her two daughters. The other daughter was former *Annie* orphan Robyn Finn, who had started with me on Broadway.

Being in East Haddam, Connecticut, was a wonderful change after the frantic pace of Broadway. Appearing in a show is hard work, of course, but my folks and I have always made it into fun, and this time was no different.

My mother and I rented a stately old house a few miles from the theater and settled in for the three-month run of the show. It was a beautiful place, set off the road on fifteen acres of land, with giant trees in front. The big backyard had a natural spring pond, and at night we'd put out salt licks, and in the morning deer and raccoons would come up to feed. With all those animals around, the house had all the comforts of my real home! My brother even came up from New Jersey one day and brought a few ducks, and for a while we had them running around the back yard.

Although the show ended in early November, we stayed up there until Thanksgiving, when my whole family showed up for dinner. There were my dad, brother, and grandparents, of course, along with my Aunt Geraldine, Uncle Otto, and cousins Rosemarie, Robin, and Laura. Laura and I were especially close because she had handled all of my fan mail when I appeared in *Annie*. With all of the other demands of the show, I didn't have time to respond to my mail personally, so Laura took over my role and wrote personal replies to everyone who wrote to me. She knew my life inside out, and whenever something came up she didn't know about, she'd ask me just to be sure she was giving the right answer. I signed and read all of the letters, but Laura was the "ghost" of Annie.

It was a beautiful warm Thanksgiving day, and while Grandma stayed inside to cook, the rest of us ran outside in our jeans for a ballgame. We were running all over the yard, which was muddy after a rainfall, when all of a sudden, Mom walked backward and fell into a giant mud hole. Everyone shrieked with delight, and my brother pulled her out sopping wet and gooey with mud. That's the way it went for the rest of the day. Soon after, we packed our bags and went home to New York for good.

My mom, Marge Merklinghaus (right) and I wait at the home of my French tutor for a lesson when I was fifteen years old. At least Babette (le chien) seems eager!

Even though the show didn't last beyond its run in Connecticut, it was a reminder to me that the theater was still very much in my blood.

On Call—and in Concert

Rarely a week went by when I wasn't asked to perform. I was always on call to sing at fund raisers for prominent politicians, such as presidential hopeful John

Connally and New York's senatorial candidate, Alphonse D'Amato. Oddly enough, they all seemed to be Republicans, and it tickled me to think it was because Daddy Warbucks was such a conservative! One week it was a political event, the next a telethon for cerebral palsy, and the next a charity dinner for an organization such as the American Cancer Society.

One of my biggest thrills was doing my own concert at a youth festival in Vancouver, Canada. The organizers of the festival had asked me to perform for the week-long event, and I quickly put together a team of talent to presentto the world the new, grown-up Shelley. Every singer needs a good back-up group, and I immediately thought of two friends of mine from New Jersey, Daniel and Carl Tramon. Carl had appeared on Broadway in *Peter Pan,* and I had known both boys for several years. Their sister, Diane, is a concert pianist and songwriter, and she arranged most of our songs.

But the format of the show was a group effort. Almost every night for a few weeks we all sat down together and brainstormed about the songs we wanted and how we wanted to put them across. We finally settled on a variety of stage hits and popular tunes, starting with an opener from *A Chorus Line,* followed by such songs as "Just the Way You Are" by Billy Joel, "You Needed Me" by Anne Murray, and "I Can't Smile Without You" by Barry Manilow. After that, came a big *Grease* routine that I would do with Daniel, and, as a grand finale, an *Annie* medley. Then, to add flair to our routines, we went to Mary Jane Houdina, the assistant to *Annie* choreographer Peter Gennaro, and asked her to put together some dance steps. For costumes, we came up with some fabulous jumpsuits made of leotard material that we could change instantaneously by snapping accessories on and off. During the *Annie* number, for instance, the boys snapped on

New York's Terence Cardinal Cooke pre-sents me with an award at one of the many appearances we made together during my year as Annie. I even sang for his birthday! Applauding at right is Mayor Abraham Beame. James Heffernan

gold lapels, put on top hats, and danced behind me as I came out in a red Annie dress singing "Tomorrow."

By the time we hit Vancouver, we had worked up a one-hour concert that we were certain would knock them dead. It did. In fact, our *Grease* segment, which we were so proud of, was almost too overwhelming for some members of the audience. They didn't seem to think a couple of fourteen-year-olds like Daniel and me should be gyrating onstage in a frenzied disco number in our tight fifties costumes. Daniel was sporting black pants and a black T-shirt, and I was looking very un-Annie-like in a racy tank top, lycra pants, and high heels.

But what really upset them was the climax of our *Grease* routine. At the end of our song medley, Daniel fell to the ground as if spurned by his "girl." I stood over him triumphantly with my arms akimbo and with an unlit cigarette dangling out of my mouth. As a final touch, I looked down at him and with the sexiest, haughtiest sneer I could muster, I said, "Tell me about it, stud."

As I said my lines, I heard some titters and uncomfortable laughter, but I didn't think much about it until after the show when the festival organizers called us on the carpet. It turns out that for better or worse, Vancouver is about ten years behind the United States in social mores, and words like "stud" are considered in bad taste. So, to make everyone happy, we dropped the word, and from then on I simply ended the routine by saying "Tell me about it."

The rest of the week we had a great time playing one show a night—and two shows on weekends—in a gigantic tent that was put up for the occasion. It was even fun when a cold spell hit and we had to muddle through with piano keys that got stuck from the cold and old-fashioned heaters to warm up the tent.

One of the things I enjoyed most was the "cool down"

period I had after the concert, when I came on stage to answer questions. One night during the cool down I was eating a green mint as one of the boys sang a song to lead into the questions. I got up to speak, and after one or two questions, one kid in the audience said boldly, "Why is your tongue green?"

Silly moments like that helped keep me from getting a swelled head about how sophisticated or successful I was. I realized that I was just another kid who had been given a special gift through my role as Annie that I could pass on to others.

In Good Voice

Wherever I went, people wanted to hear "Tomorrow." That one song had captured the hearts of people everywhere and tapped a sense of hope and life deep within them. Each time I sang it, no matter what the crowd or how big the audience, people would cheer and clap with an excitement that sent shivers down my spine. It thrilled me to know that I had a talent I could still share with people. And the more I sang, the more I sensed that day by day, my voice was growing and maturing as I left my girlhood behind.

As the months went on, I also discovered that my career aspirations didn't have to be limited to Broadway. I auditioned for a small role in the horror movie The Burning, and in the summer of 1980 I found myself in a Boy Scout Camp in North Tonowanda, New York, making a movie!

On Film

There were no big stars in the film—just a group of young actors and actresses like me who played the parts of kids at a summer camp. My role was that of "Tiger," a tomboy type who was the youngest camper in the senior cabin. Although I wasn't a lead character, I had little scenes throughout the whole movie. Actually, I was more famous than I realized at the time. Recently, the movie appeared on cable TV, and I was shocked to see that the program notes in the cable-TV guide listed me as one of the stars!

The story of the movie centered around the revenge of a man who as a camp counselor many years before had been cruelly tricked by the campers in his charge. He was a mean, nasty person, and as a prank one night, the kids had stuck a candle in an old wormy skull and put it near his bed. Then to wake him, they made eerie sounds at his window. The man, drunk in his bed, woke up in horror, and in a crazed stupor he knocked over the skull and the candle set the cabin on fire. Everything went up in flames, and he struggled to open the door, finally bursting through with his body aflame.

"I'll get my revenge," he screamed.

Years later, another group of kids, including my character, was at the same camp, sitting around the campfire telling stories, when the man returned like a ghost to wreak his revenge. After terrorizing the campers, the man ultimately met his death.

The movie wasn't another *Annie* by a long shot, but it was a chance for me to get my feet wet as a movie actress. The only other movie I had ever made was the *The Godfather*, and my two days as an extra at age seven couldn't compare to the experience of spending three weeks shooting *The Burning* as a teenager.

One thing I learned from *The Burning* was that making movies is a lot easier in some ways than being on stage. Even though we had to shoot two versions of certain scenes—one for the screen and one with toned-down language for television—there was plenty of free time in-between scenes. Sometimes all the standing around and reshooting could get boring, but I was used to that because of my previous work with commercials.

Broadway, on the other hand, is *constant*. It's not just a one-shot deal where you shoot a film and a few weeks later move on to something else. In the theater, you have to be ready to get up and perform day in and day out for the run of the show. Lately, a lot of movie stars have come under attack for their absenteeism and lack of commitment to Broadway roles they've taken on, and now I can understand the problem. The stars who have made their marks in other media simply aren't used to the relentless demands of the stage. It wasn't by accident, I guess, that the byword "the show must go on" grew up in the theater and not the movies.

What Next?

By the time I turned sixteen, in May 1981, I was ready for a bigger challenge. I knew it wasn't Broadway—after all, there was no other role like Annie, and I wasn't ready yet to get back on that kind of nonstop schedule. But I was ready to work, and work hard. My thoughts turned to TV pilots or maybe even another movie, and I approached each day eagerly and expectantly, hoping that a new opportunity was just around the corner.

But it was not to be.

My fantasies were shattered just one month later on that terrifying June morning when I awoke in agony from a pain in my back. After a hospitalization that nearly killed me and tests that were inconclusive, the mysterious pain disappeared just as rapidly as it had come. I spent the summer free of pain and feeling like my old self. The juices had started to flow in me again, and I was excited by the prospect of a good year at school and the untold possibilities for me in show business.

But, once again, pain and discomfort struck—this time more terrifying than before. I was told I had leukemia—a disease that was so horrifying in its implications that even the word itself made me cringe in fear. One day I was at home suffering from what I thought was a simple virus. That night, I found myself in a hospital room next to a dying baby in the world's most famous cancer center, Memorial Sloan-Kettering.

During those first few weeks in the hospital, I had tried—oh how I had tried—to keep up my spirits and keep myself going, just as I had on Broadway night after night. The most important thing you learn in show business is that the show must go on—at all costs. If I could go on the stage, as I had as an understudy, so sick that I was falling down and still give a show-stopping performance, I could *will* myself to persevere through this crisis too. At least, that's what I told myself. So, I forced myself to go to the hospital playroom to practice my scales, only to be totally beaten down when I couldn't hit any of the notes.

But I didn't quit that easily. Like a Broadway trouper, I went back again to the playroom another night in the vain hope that I could pull it off. That's when I had tried to sing "Tomorrow" and got nothing but squeaks. And that's when I ran out of the playroom, convinced that I would never sing again—and without any hope that I would ever walk out of the hospital alive.

Cobwebs and Sorrow

I raced from the playroom, down the empty hall of the pediatrics unit and finally to my room, where I threw myself on the bed, sobbing. The little baby, Yolanda, and her mother were fast asleep in the bed next to mine, and I tried to muffle my sobs so I wouldn't wake them.

Life was so unfair. Why was this happening to me? What *was* happening to me? My voice was gone, my body was falling apart on the inside, and there was nothing I could do about it. Nothing.

I could feel the walls of my room closing in on me. During the day, the room danced with cheerful cards, balloons, and stuffed animals sent by friends and fans. But now, shrouded in the darkness of midnight, the room seemed frightening as those tokens of love were transformed into shadowy monsters. Even my favorite present a huge parrot-faced mask that had been given to me in the hospital by Peter Gennaro, the choreographer of *Annie*, appeared ugly and grotesque. From every corner I could feel strange eyes looking at me and eerie shapes and forms jumping out at me as a horrible reminder of the nightmare I was living through.

Yolanda and Kenny

My mind raced as I thought of all the misery that surrounded me. There was little Yolanda, of course, who was only fourteen months old and too young to fully comprehend all that she was suffering. But somehow she must have understood, because she never ever tried to babble or talk like other kids her age. She just cried all the time. She cried when they tried to give her a bath or when anyone tried to touch her.

At first, she wouldn't let mom or me hold her either; but after a while, she would let us take her in our arms and talk to her. She was so precious—a little peanut with big round beautiful eyes that always seemed to be filled with sadness. Nothing seemed to take away that distant, frightened look in her eyes. One of the male nurses came in every day and wheeled her around the floor in a little red wagon. He'd prop her up with pillows, and with her IV pole rolling along behind, off she'd go. But even then, she never smiled.

Would that be my fate too?

A few doors away from me was a five-year-old girl who was doing great until she contracted pneumonia. She died quietly one night as she slept.

Then there was little Kenny, a bright four-year-old who celebrated his birthday with a party in the hospital playroom. It was a wonderful party. All the kids brought little gifts, and we all carried on as though there would be dozens of birthdays ahead.

A few night later, though, Kenny's dad poked his head into my room.

"How's Kenny doing?" I asked brightly.

"He just had a bone scan," the father said. And then, mustering all the courage he had, he poured out the tragic results. "He has a tumor over 95 percent of his body."

I sat there stunned. What touched me even more was that the man had told us so matter-of-factly, without even shedding a tear. I don't know whether his stoicism was for my benefit or for his own. But he had just told me in so many words that his son was hopeless. The dear little boy with the cherubic smile who had happily blown out four candles "and one to grow on" a few days before was going to die.

That's the way it went in the pediatric unit. Behind each door was a story more heartrending than the next. As I lay in my bed, consumed with my sorrows, I couldn't erase these terrible images from my mind. Whenever a positive thought came into my head, it would quickly be pushed out by the fears and anxiety and pain I was feeling.

The Chances for Survival

Every now and then a ray of hope would creep in when I tried to pull myself back from self-pity and think rationally about my chances.

My doctors had said I was suffering from acute lymphoblastic leukemia, the most common form of childhood leukemia. In practical terms, my body was producing an inordinate number of abnormal white blood cells, which were dividing like crazy and crowding out the normal blood cells necessary for a healthy life. Until every single cancerous cell was destroyed and normal blood cell formation resumed, I would be weak and highly susceptible to all kinds of infections.

The cure rate for this type of leukemia was said to be between 65 and 75 percent—which meant that at least 65 percent of those who are treated make it. What's more, those who live more than five years have a greater than 95 percent chance of living a long and healthy life.

The really positive news was that for me or for any individual with the disease, the chances for survival were, in a sense, either zero or one hundred. In other words, I'd either be one of the 65 percent who were winners, or one of the losers, and either way it would be all the way. So, I could keep feeling depressed and think I'd have no chance of making it, or I could keep up my spirits and expect to be completely cured.

Maybe I'd be one of the lucky ones, like Danny, a beautiful, raven-haired girl my age who had visited me the day I checked into the hospital. Danny had come to Memorial for her annual checkup, and while she was in my room talking to me, her father took my parents outside to share his experiences.

Danny told me how she had gotten cancer when she was eleven—the age I was when I opened in *Annie* on Broadway. While I was kicking up my heels on stage, she had been close to death in Memorial. Yet, here she was, five years later, looking gorgeous and vibrant and full of life.

If Danny had made it, I could too. I had every reason to be hopeful. But no matter how hard I tried to believe it, I just couldn't—not at this stage, anyway. I could see no tangible evidence that I was getting any better. The only

---

With my arm hooked up to an IV tube, I'm trying to put on a happy face during my first weeks of hospitalization at Memorial Sloan-Kettering Cancer Center. Next to me is a book of puzzles, which I pored over until the wee hours of the morning, and an order of Chinese food I had delivered. © *by Harry Hamburg*

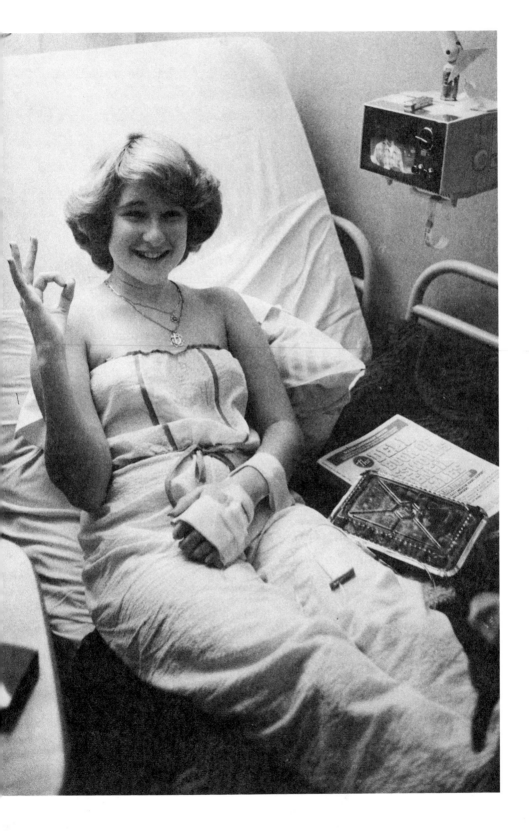

effect of the disease I saw was that it had destroyed the most precious part of me—my voice.

A Search and Destroy Mission

Actually, it wasn't the leukemia that had affected my singing, it was the chemotherapy—combinations of potent drugs I was taking to attack the disease. One theory about leukemia is that the disease begins with one single cancerous cell that reproduces and spreads throughout the body. In order to fight the leukemia successfully, it's necessary to eradicate every last leukemic cell.

During my first weeks in the hospital, my doctors were literally waging a search and destroy mission in my body. The "general" leading this mission was Dr. Michael Sorell, a pediatric oncologist who was the assistant director of Memorial's pediatric day hospital. He was in charge of my case during my hospitalization. Dr. Murphy, who had given me entree to the hospital, was to follow me as an outpatient after I was discharged.

Under Dr. Sorell's direction, I was taking antibiotics to knock out infection and a battery of anticancer drugs to attack the leukemia on several fronts. My arm seemed permanently attached to an IV tube, which provided antibiotics as well as a constant flow of fluids into my body to speed up elimination of wastes generated by the drugs.

What made my condition even more complicated was that a few days after entering the hospital, I developed diabetes as a result of taking the hormone prednisone. That meant that on top of all the other drugs I was taking, I also had to take insulin to bring my diabetes under control. I learned how to give myself insulin shots by practicing first on an orange. Then I practiced on the arm of one of the nurses. Three times a day before meals, I'd get a blood test to determine how much insulin I needed, and then I'd go to the pharmacy down the hall, get the insulin, clean off the bottle, draw the insulin up in the needle, and inject myself. My arm was covered with black and blue marks from all of the blood tests and injections.

In a healthy person, the normal blood sugar level is around 110, but mine had soared up to 700. Unfortunately, even with the insulin, my blood sugar wasn't coming down as fast as it should have, and my doctors were beginning to get concerned. I felt weak a lot of the time and even had trouble walking some days because I simply had no strength. Because of my slow progress in those first weeks of treatment, my doctors feared that even if I came through the leukemia, I might have diabetes for the rest of my life.

I wish I could say that, like Annie, I bore up under all of this by sticking out my chin and looking optimistically toward tomorrow. But the squeaks in my voice that night in the playroom had burst whatever bubble of hope I had, and I withdrew into a shell.

Hospital Routine

In the days afterward I turned my back on the active—even joyful—life of the hospital that was going on outside my door. As difficult as it is to believe, there was joy all around me at Memorial, whether or not I chose to share in it. In the pediatric unit the hospital had created a world that was as comfortable, loving, and full of fun as it could possibly be. From my room I could hear the corridors resound with squeals of delight as kids raced down the halls at breakneck speed while balanced on their IV poles, which had wheels attached to them. Never once did I hear a nurse yell at a kid for going too fast or for getting into mischief. They yelled at the doctors, maybe, but never at the kids.

The nurses must have all been chosen from a group of

special angels sent down from heaven for the purpose of ministering to our needs, because their devotion to us was out of this world. If anyone said, "I need you" or "I want you," they were there in a minute. And they seemed to have endless hours of time to talk, to sit quietly by the bedside, or to joke around.

My friend Maureen Dwyer, the nurse who let me into the playroom to vocalize, used to come in at night and tell mom and me about her adventures. She had traveled all around the world, and she'd regale me for hours with her stories. Another nurse named JoAnne would stay up with me until long past midnight, doing puzzles. My mom would sometimes fall asleep before I did, but I always had someone to share those late sleepless hours.

Once, a doctor came in and reprimanded JoAnne for keeping me up. "We have a schedule to uphold in this hospital," he said gruffly. "Certain children have to go to bed at a certain time."

But after he left, she just shrugged, and we continued with our puzzle.

Every few days, a wonderful volunteer, Lola, would come into the room to try to entice me to the playroom, where all sorts of activities were planned. "We're going to bake cookies now, Shelley," she'd say. Or, "We're going to make some jewelry. Come on."

But I just shook my head. I wanted no part of "pizza night" or "cookie night" or "Las Vegas night"—or any other night. To my way of thinking, these were just diversions aimed at keeping our minds occupied with positive thoughts. What was the use of keeping busy? Why stand side by side with another kid at a Las Vegas night and win prizes and cheer and smile and pretend that everything was coming up roses when you might not even be here the next week?

What really drove me crazy was the thought of having

to cheer someone else up. Many times, other kids on the floor would drop by to say hello. Inevitably, they would end up explaining why they were in the hospital and what they were going through. I was a great listener. But I'll have to admit that I wasn't much for conversation. I was having too much trouble coping with my ownproblems to be genuinely interested in responding supportively to someone else's woes.

Saying It with Flowers

Since I wasn't emotionally able to share myself with the other kids, I reached out the only way I knew how—by sending them some of the flowers that filled my room. Thanks to my friends and dozens of loyal fans, my room always looked like a florist shop. It was my grandmother who showed me a way to give of myself, even when I couldn't do it in person. She always spent some time every day in the room set aside for parents with the other parents and their kids. I never went with her, because I knew the scene would be too heavy. But she'd come back crying for the people she had met and the problems they were facing. "They have no flowers, Shelley," she'd say.

And so, I'd send her out—like a FTD messenger—with bouquets and floral arrangements for everyone who needed some good cheer. Before long, my flowers were everywhere, and everyone knew my grandmother's face.

My mother provided the same kind of sunny presence. No matter how down in the dumps I was, she always managed to remain upbeat and positive. Even though she was often torn apart inside, she never let it show. She'd do her crying outside my room and reserve her best moments for me. She stayed at my bedside day in and day out, around the clock, sharing my pain, just as she had shared my triumph with *Annie*.

In her warm, cajoling way, she was on my back at every turn, urging me to get on with life and enjoy myself. I used to hang around my room in my pajamas, even though I could have put on street clothes, and she tried as hard as she could to get me into a pair of jeans.

Every day Mom would say, "Why don't you get out of these pajamas and put on some clothes?" And every day, I'd give the same answer.

"I don't want to—why should I?" I'd reply, and I'd stay in my pajamas for one more day. There really wasn't any reason to get dressed. I couldn't go anywhere, and the clothes made me think even more how I was stuck in the hospital and couldn't get out.

If my big hang-up was being confined, my mother's was cleanliness. She was a fanatic about the subject. Every night, after everybody had left the room, she'd scrub my room down with a disinfectant. She'd do the whole room—the floors, the walls, the chairs, the bed— anything anyone from outside had touched.

She was like my shield against germs. My white blood count—the body's natural infection fighters in the bloodstream—often went very low, and when that happened, I was vulnerable to every single germ. Mom didn't give those germs any quarter. Outside the room she put a big sign saying, "Wash your hands," and inside another one just like it was the first thing that hit you.

It may have seemed crazy—but you do crazy things when you're desperate. I'll have to admit it embarrassed me a little, but then, I wasn't about to take any chances.

Mom was also my first line of defense against the doctors, who came around every morning like clockwork. Memorial is a teaching hospital, and, of course, the physicians made rounds every day to examine the patients and discuss cases with the interns and residents. But I had managed to get through two years on Broadway without undressing completely in front of someone else, and there was no way I was going to be examined in front of all those young doctors!

So, I'd wait until I could hear the doctors in the next room, and then I'd run into the bathroom and hide.

"There goes Shelley," Mom would say, laughing.

When the physicians came in the room, inevitably the bed would be empty, and Mom would make my excuse. "I'm sorry, Shelley's in the bathroom," she'd say. Or, "You missed her again, doctors."

As soon as they moved on to the next room, she'd tap on the door to tell me the coast was clear. Our ploy was so successful that during my entire stay in the hospital, I think I was examined only once or twice on morning rounds.

I never realized until my illness how very much I needed my mother. Of course, she had been with me at every step of my career, waiting in the wings while I was onstage, driving me to New York every day, and making sure I made it to appointments and appearances at all hours of the day and night. Without her, I could never have been a star on Broadway.

But this was different. This time I needed not only her physical presence and her supportive words; I needed every ounce of her spirit, and I drew on it time and time again. When I felt too low even to pray, she'd be there pleading with God for me. And the strength she got from those moments enabled her to keep giving to me every single moment.

One morning I woke up writhing in pain. The feeling was all too familiar—exactly like the pain that had hit me on that June day a few months earlier when I was rushed to the hospital for tests.

As it turned out, my bowels were blocked up as a result of some of the medication I was taking. But whatever the cause, the pain was horrendous. Mom begged one of the residents to let her give me some mineral oil, but the doctor refused. The next day, I was still doubled over in pain, and finally, Mom's persistence won the day. I was given an enema, and for an entire day, Mom sat in bed with me, holding my head on her lap like a real-life Pietà. All day long she fed me little sips of tea and stroked my head, assuring me that all would be well. Gradually, the pain subsided, and a few days later I was back to normal—at least as normal as I could be in a cancer hospital.

Self-Hypnosis

During the day, I'd try to appear upbeat, especially when my family and friends came to visit, which they did almost every day. My grandparents and my dad were there every night. Dad would usually stick around until about twelve-thirty to make sure I had everything I needed, and afterward he'd take home my laundry, wash it, and bring it back clean the next day. No matter what I needed, and no matter what time of the day or night it was, he'd manage to get it for me. Fortunately, he's a sales manager for Dynamit-Nobel, a German corporation founded by Alfred Nobel, and his job was flexible enough to give him the time to be with me. But what touched me so deeply was his willingness to do *my* dirty work.

Along with Dad and the rest of my family, my friend JoAnn would be there every night to keep me company. At other times Andrea and other friends from the show would stop by. We'd hang out in the playroom and have a lot of laughs. But when they went home, and I was alone with my mom, I'd retreat behind the emotional wall I had built up around me.

My wall began to crumble a couple of weeks after I entered the hospital. It all started with my second bone-marrow test and spinal injection on November 4. The tests promised to be painful—and they *were* painful. But somehow the pain wasn't as intense as I remembered from those first two days in the hospital. Maybe it was because I knew what was coming and was more relaxed. Another thing that helped was that I had worked with a special hospital psychologist on self-hypnosis techniques. In just a few sessions he had taught me how to relax in stressful situations. He said I should try to imagine myself in a very comfortable place that was soothing and restful and focus completely on that.

As a result, as the bone marrow was being taken from my hipbone, I pictured myself in a pool of water with sunlight beating down on me and steam coming off the water. The image was so real that I could almost feel the warmth of the sun and the steam, and my body relaxed in response. This time the bone-marrow test only took about ten seconds, compared to eight minutes on my first day in the hospital, because they only needed a small amount of fluid.

My self-hypnosis had worked so well that I repeated it during the spinal injection, a painful procedure that involves putting a needle between the bones of the spine to inject medicine into the spinal fluid. That was the only way they could be sure that no leukemic cells were in the central nervous system, which cannot be reached by ordinary chemotherapy that circulates through the bloodstream.

Thirsty for Hope

As Dr. Sorell carried out the procedure, I relaxed again, and before I knew it, I was up and ready to go back to my room. *This isn't so bad, after all,* I thought to myself. *I can live with this.*

To top it off, the results from the test were immediate. Dr. Sorell stuck a slide of marrow under the microscope and came into my room with a smile on his face. "It looks good," he said.

I said a silent prayer of thanks, and when I went back to my room, I scribbled in a little black diary: "Thank you dear Lord."

Just the simple act of being thankful made me feel even more positive about my situation. I wasn't out of the woods yet, but I could sense that already I had changed. I was more receptive to hearing the words of encouragement so many people had tried to offer me during the last two weeks. Like a dry sponge that is ready to soak up any available drop of water, I was thirsty for hope and life.

An Important Postscript

The very next day, November 5, a letter came in the mail that boosted my spirits even more. It was from Mayor Koch, and his words helped bring me face to face with my own strengths and showed me what I needed to do to come out of Memorial a star:

> Seven million New Yorkers join me in telling you that we love you and we want you to get better. Please comply with this request as soon as possible.
>
> We know you can. After all, you've done everything else in your life so exceptionally well and with such tremendous flair . . .
>
> Shelley, if you have to be in a hospital, you are in one of the best in the world. But, nonetheless, get out of that hospital soon.

As I read his letter, I grew more and more confident that I would make it. In my mind I could almost picture those seven million New Yorkers he was talking about, walking the sidewalks, clogging its streets in cars and buses and subways. The city pulsed with life, and I could feel that life force beckoning me to be part of the action again.

What echoed in my mind, though, was his supreme confidence in me. "We know you can do it," he had said.

But what really hit home, and made me realize what I had to do beginning right then and there, was his hand-written postscript, scrawled in black ink at the bottom of the letter.

"Remember," wrote the Mayor, "we both *perform*."

He was right. I was an actress—a performer—someone who could live another role as though it were real. No matter what the outcome was for me, I had to play this role to the hilt. Up to now I was playing my role as a victim who was slowly being destroyed by forces beyond her control. But there was another way to play the role. I could play it like Annie and be the master of my fate and emerge triumphant.

Symbol of Freedom

As if to confirm my new attitude toward life, that very day I received a visible sign of my improvement: I was unhooked from my IV tube, which almost seemed to have become a part of my body. To me, that simple change in my life was a symbol of the freedom I felt to turn away from fear and embrace the future with hope.

I felt like celebrating! My very first thought was to share my excitement with Andrea, who had planned to drop by that afternoon before she headed for the St. Regis Hotel, where she was appearing in a show. It was her eighteenth birthday, and to surprise her, I ordered up the richest chocolate cake you could ever imagine. It was a five-layer cake, smeared with gooey chocolate on every layer and smothered in shredded chocolate.

Andrea was thrilled that I had remembered, and for the rest of the day, we giggled and talked as though I had never been in the hospital at all. I was euphoric without my IV pole, and we raced to the playroom and hung out in music room, which was filled with drums, a piano, an organ, a stereo, and even a pinball machine. For what seemed like hours, we hopped from the instruments to the pinball machine and back to the instruments again, holding a two-girl jam session.

Another Try at the Tapes

By the time Andrea left for the show, I was riding such a wave that I felt as if I could do *anything*. So, that very night, I decided to pull out my tapes and try to sing again. It was the first time since losing my voice that I had gotten up the courage to sing, and I have to admit I was a little afraid that my voice would still be out of control. But, strangely enough, I was more afraid of *not* going, and I found myself propelled toward the playroom by a tremendous sense of confidence.

To my surprise, I did one tape that night, and my voice didn't even squeak! A couple of nights later, I did another tape, and then I went back again the following night to sing some more. The more I sang, the more I wanted to keep singing on and on and on.

My body wasn't yet ready to keep pace with my spirits though, and over the next couple of days I felt weak and a little queasy. But even that didn't get me down, because I knew that I had too much going for me to give in to a little sickness. I began to take a new interest in everything that was going on around me at the hospital. I started spending a lot of time at the pharmacy, asking the pharmacists

Andrea McArdle, who originated the role of Annie on Broadway, shares a laugh with me in my room at Memorial. On the wall behind me are some of the 600 cards and letters I received from fans during my forty-two days in the hospital. © *by Harry Hamburg*

to explain all about the drugs I was using. I was so fascinated by the work I thought maybe after I graduated from high school I might go on to pharmacy school. Little by little, I found myself enjoying the other patients more, and I even made it to the playroom for Las Vegas night.

A Reason to Be Positive

On November 18, nearly a month after I entered the hospital, I had my third bone-marrow test and spinal injection. As I walked to the examining room, my heart was pounding with anticipation. What would the tests reveal? Would there be any improvement? I hoped and prayed that I was indeed getting better and that my good spirits weren't just the result of my wishful thinking.

But I had an even more important reason to try to be positive that day. Tagging along by my side was an entourage of little kids who wanted to listen outside the door as I was being tested. One of the children, a seven-year-old named Anthony, was scared about going for a bone-marrow test, and when he heard I was due for mine he begged to come along.

"I'll wait outside," he said imploringly, and I couldn't turn him down.

I left the kids at the door and went inside for my tests and treatment, hoping against hope that everything would turn out okay. But for some reason, the injections were unusually painful that day. I tried the self-hypnosis techniques I had learned, but the thoughts of the warm sun and pools of water couldn't diminish the pain. The doctor had to stick me three times for the spinal, and even though he assured me that this was common, with each probe I grew more and more upset. By the time the needle was inserted properly, I was ready to scream. But I knew I couldn't make a peep, because the little kids were right outside the door, listening.

If I cry or yell out, those kids will really get frightened, I thought. You *can't* give up now, Shelley, I told myself.

By some miracle, I drew on my last vestige of self-restraint and kept my mouth shut. But inside, I was in agony. How long would I have to endure this, I wondered? How long could I keep on being hopeful when it hurt so much?

I didn't have to wait long. Soon after the tests, the doctor from the lab stuck his head in the door of my room. His whole face was lit up in a smile, and the minute I saw him, I knew I was going to be okay.

"You're in remission, Shelley!" he said.

I let out a scream of joy, and before I knew it, my mom and the doctor and I were all hugging and laughing and hugging some more. According to the tests, there was no sign of cancer in my body—anywhere. It didn't mean that I was free of cancer for all time. I knew the facts—that I could come out of remission at any time, without warning. But I wasn't about to fill my mind with negative thoughts, especially about things that might never happen. All I could think about was that at that moment—and maybe even *forever*—I was free of the disease.

Suddenly, everything around me seemed to surge with life. I started to daydream about what I'd do after I left the hospital and about how I couldn't wait to see my cat, Fidi, and sit in my grandmother's kitchen, eating some of her special zeppoles.

In my diary that night, my mom wrote in giant letters: REMISSION! YEA! THANK YOU GOD. It was unbelievable but true. I had *won* the first part of the battle!

Final Treatment

The very next day I was scheduled to begin the second stage of therapy, a series of ten radiation treatments and additional spinal injections, aimed at preventing a recurrence of the disease. The treatments were simply an insurance policy—to prevent even one little malignant cell from arising in my central nervous system. Soon, very soon, I'd be out the door of the hospital and on my way to living my life again.

My doctors had explained that radiation was simply an x-ray, given in low doses for a minute or so. The treatment, they said, would be painless—just like the x-rays I had taken in my dentist's office. Afterward, I would experience some side effects—such as a loss of hair—but eventually they would pass.

At this point, I was in a good frame of mind because I knew my cancer was on the way out. But I still wasn't completely prepared for everything that was about to happen to me in this final stage of treatment. The next morning I was wheeled downstairs to Machine Room 242, where a monstrous machine that could have been featured in *Star Wars* silently blasted my head with x-rays. As I started up from the x-ray table, I was so nervous that I fell off the table onto my knees. Later that afternoon, I broke out in a sweat, my eyes started to tingle, and my body trembled all over.

Over the next few days, as I had additional treatments, I felt like I was on a roller coaster of physical and mental discomfort. One day I'd hear funny noises in my ears and be grouchy all day, while the next day I'd be chipper and feel just fine. When the going got rough, though, as crummy as I felt, I'd remember that my suffering would soon be over. I might be shaking and sweating on the outside, but *inside* my body was free of leukemia. That was all that really mattered—or so I thought.

Side Effects

But then something happened that shook me to the very core of my being and made me question the faith I had in my recovery. I had been warned to expect certain inevitable side effects of the radiation and chemotherapy, but I didn't want to admit it could happen to me.

So, I ignored the warning signs, until one night in mid-November, when I couldn't run away from the truth any longer.

Laughter filled the room that night, and as I looked around at my mom and dad, my grandparents, and my friend Shirley Hoffman, who worked with *Annie* producer Lewis Allen, I got a little shiver up my spine, thinking about how lucky I was to have so many people to love.

I leaned back in bed, letting my head rest against the religious medals sent by fans, which covered the headboard. My mother had taped them there to give us all a sense that someone was watching over me. And so far, at least, someone was.

But as I pulled away from the headboard, I felt a little tug at my hair, and I turned around to see some hair stuck on one of the medals. Oh well, I thought, that could have happened anytime.

But deep inside, another thought was eating away at me. During the past few weeks, I had become aware that something very strange was happening to my body. I'd put my hand up to my head to brush away a lock of hair, and somehow my hair would just feel different. Or, I'd brush my hair and look down afterward to see a clump entangled in the bristles.

I didn't have to look in a mirror to know what was going on. I could just *feel* it. My beautiful hair, which had once been my crowning glory, was slowly falling out.

At first I had tried to dismiss it by telling myself, What's the big deal—it's gonna grow back. But day by day, as my hair grew thinner and thinner, it was more difficult to rationalize. I felt strange—as though I were somebody else. It just wasn't *me*. I knew it didn't make sense, but there was no way to explain to anyone how I felt.

"Don't brush my hair tonight," I said to my mom. But she wouldn't listen. She started brushing it, and as she brushed, I could feel the hair falling on my back. With every brush stroke, more and more hair fell out. Finally, I couldn't take it anymore, and I burst into tears. When I tried to explain it to my mom, she tried to shrug it off.

"But you don't understand," I shouted. With that, I ran into the bathroom and slammed the door. She wouldn't let me alone. She followed me right into the bathroom and called through the door for everyone to leave. Then, with me perched on the lid of the toilet seat and her on the edge of the bathtub, she gave me a dose of her no-nonsense, lay-it-on-the-table advice that had kept me going through the ups and downs of *Annie*.

"You know what, Shelley," she said with a touch of irony in her voice, "maybe it would have been better if you were dead and had hair, rather than alive with no hair."

Her words were perfectly logical, but I wasn't interested in logic. I was sixteen, and there was no way I could accept life on those terms. I only wanted to be *me*— the way I was before I ever set foot in Memorial Hospital. Nothing I said could make her understand how I felt, and all I could do was bury my face in my hands, wondering when it would all be over.

PART THREE

7

A Time for Thanksgiving

"I feel like I'm in prison," I wailed to Dr. Fenner, a handsome young resident who had stopped in to find out how I was doing. With my eyes searching his face for some sign of hope, I begged him to let me out just for one hour.

"Can't I go home—just for a little while?" I pleaded.

I knew what his answer would be even before the words were out of his mouth. Although there were no bars to hold me, there was no escape from the relentless routine of the hospital. He told me that my leukemia treatment was going well, but until the diabetes I had gotten from the anticancer drugs was under control, I couldn't be released from the hospital.

As he explained why he couldn't let me go, something in his eyes told me that he understood my hurt and frustration. What amazed me even more was that he didn't just say his piece and leave. Instead, he sat down by my bed, and for one solid hour he talked to me gently, reassuring me that I'd be going home soon.

"Be patient, Shelley," he said. "It's only a matter of time."

I had needed something to cling to, and his certainty became my lifeline. After he left that day, I found myself relaxing, and before long I was waiting expectantly for the day I could go home. Every night as I went to bed, I'd think to myself, Maybe it will even be tomorrow!

Ethiopian Princess

Each day, the sun seemed to shine more brightly through my little window, now that I knew I was going home. What helped the time to fly by was a little Ethiopian girl named Tareika, who came into my life quite suddenly. Tiny Yolanda and her mom were moved to a corner room, which they had wanted for some time, and into the bed next to mine hopped an adorable four-year-old. She immediately captured my heart, and soon I was thinking more about her than about myself.

Tareika had come into the hospital a week before I did, and now, like me, she was in remission and counting the days until she could go home. Because her mom worked, she was alone much of the time, but we quickly took her under our wing.

Tareika was like a little princess, with a matching outfit for every day of the week. If she had on a pink nightgown, she'd be sure to put on her pink slippers, pink bathrobe, and pink bows in the thin little wisps that remained of her hair.

Tareika had an air about her that commanded love and attention. She was like a little administrator—walking all over the pediatric wing, poking her nose in everyone's room to see how they were doing, and hanging out at the nurses' station.

There was no way you could be anything but positive with Tareika around. I liked to joke that she was four going on forty-four, because you couldn't put anything past her. Her impish sense of humor would keep us all in stitches. We'd be in the middle of a conversation and out of the blue she'd give a devilish look and say, "You banana head."

The Best Thanksgiving Ever

Everything about her reminded me of joy and hope, and I was so grateful for her presence. With each passing day, her indomitable spirit spilled over into mine, and I could feel my heart overflowing with optimism. Thanksgiving was just a few days away, and I could tell that for me it would be the best Thanksgiving ever.

Grandma had suggested that we take it easy on Thanksgiving and simply call out for Chinese food. But I couldn't imagine celebrating the most important Thanksgiving of my life over a plate of fried rice. I wanted a real, honest-to-goodness home-cooked banquet, just like the one we would have had at home, and I appealed to my grandmother for help.

"Grandma," I said, "I *can't* call out for Thanksgiving dinner. It's not right."

"All right," she relented. "I'll make you anything you want." She made a list and I went to bed dreaming of the stuffed mushrooms and turkey and cranberry sauce she would carry in from her kitchen.

I had even more to be thankful for on Thanksgiving than I realized. When I awoke Thanksgiving morning, tests showed that for the first time since I entered the hospital, my blood sugar was normal, and I was taken off insulin. My diabetes was finally under control! Now, it was only a matter of days before I'd be going home.

The first thing I did was take off my pajamas and put on a pair of jeans. I had dropped from 102 to 88 pounds in the hospital, and the jeans, which had once been too tight, fit me like a dream. A few hours later, my room started to fill up with family and friends who had come to celebrate the Thanksgiving feast. Mom and Dad were there, of course, along with my brother, JoAnn, my grandparents, Andrea, Shirley Hoffman, and Tareika and her mother.

Grandma had brought in platters laden with turkey and all the trimmings, which we placed on a rickety table at one end of the room. Then, balancing plates on our laps, we sat on the beds, chairs, and floor to eat our meal.

But we couldn't begin eating before remembering the source of our thankful hearts. As a hush fell over the room, Tareika offered the traditional Catholic blessing: "Bless us, oh Lord," she said, "through these thy gifts." She paused, forgetting the rest of the prayer, and looked at me to pick up her lines. "Which we are about to receive from thy bounty," I said. "Through Jesus Christ, our Lord, Amen."

As I said the words of the grace, I knew that I had already received the most important gift—the gift of life. The meal I was about to eat was simply a confirmation of the life God had already given me. This Thanksgiving meal, made by my grandmother's hands, was the "daily bread" He had promised to provide one day at a time as I needed it.

In my heart I knew that I didn't have to worry about the future anymore. All I had to do was live my life as best I could, one day at a time. If I could do that with all my heart, every day would truly be Thanksgiving.

My big brother, Jimmy, and I at home with our cat, Fidi, and dog, Babette after my hospitalization at Memorial Hospital. Mary McLoughlin—N.Y. Post

Within days, both Tareika and I got to go home. She left a couple of days after Thanksgiving, and on November 30, 1981, forty-two days after entering the hospital, I walked out of Memorial Sloan-Kettering Cancer Center, ready to begin my life again. In my hand was a small unicorn my mom had given me to symbolize my hard-won victory.

I didn't actually walk right out of the hospital. Rather, my mom and I sneaked out like a couple of bandits because I didn't want the news media to know. Ever since the word had leaked out that I was hospitalized, I had been deluged with requests for interviews. But I couldn't have handled a lot of publicity at the time, and the hospital had simply issued a press release explaining my treatment and had referred all questions to my doctors. I was apparently such a hot item that special news bulletins on my hospitalization cut into regular TV and radio programming.

Press Conference

Now that I was out of the hospital, though, I couldn't hold off the press much longer. I was smart enough to realize that I needed a couple of days to adjust to my new life at home, and so I waited until I returned to the hospital for my final radiation treatment a few days later to hold a press conference.

I thought I had known what it was like to be a celebrity when I starred in *Annie*. But the attention I received on Broadway paled in comparison to the interest I generated as a cancer patient. When my press conference was announced for December 3, the hospital was swamped with calls from TV stations and newspapers wanting to send reporters and camera crews.

I couldn't believe the response, and as I walked

toward the hospital banquet room, where the press conference was being held, I found myself musing on the irony of my situation. I had never had a press conference of my own as Annie, but now everybody wanted to hear my story.

"You know, Mom," I said, laughing, "I couldn't have *paid* for all the publicity I'm getting!"

Light bulbs started flashing the minute I walked in the room, and even though this was my first time alone on the firing line, I wasn't at all nervous. It was actually a lot easier to stand before a roomful of reporters from every major TV station, newspaper, and wire service in the city, than to get up on stage. I simply treated the event like any other interview and started fielding questions.

"What did you think of the first time you thought you were going to die?" asked a woman reporter.

Oddly enough, I didn't feel any emotion at all as she hit me bluntly with the question that must have been on everybody's mind. My only thought was that I was up there doing a job. There was no time for feelings, only for straightforward answers.

"I did think of that at first," I replied, "but after it was explained to me, I was fine."

I wasn't always fine, of course, but the ups and downs of my emotions in the hospital were too complicated to explain in a short press conference. During the next half hour I tried my best to project the confidence and optimism I was genuinely feeling at that moment and to explain what was ahead of me.

Soon, I explained, I'd be moving into the final stage of treatment called "maintenance therapy," where for two years or more I'd be taking chemotherapy at home and returning to the hospital as an outpatient once a month for a chemotherapy shot and every three months for a bone-marrow test and spinal tap. I wasn't strong enough yet to return to school or to resume my career, but as for next year, I said, "We'll just see."

The one question I feared most—about my hair— never came up, probably because I had hidden my thin wisps under a chic beige beret. Although there was never a time during or after my hospitalization when I was *totally* without hair, I was still sensitive about it. My head was covered with very fine long wisps, and in between were short bristles where the hair I had lost was growing in.

Hat Trick

In the hospital I had been so obsessed with my hair that I wouldn't look in a mirror. In fact, I did everything I could to avoid facing the truth. Whenever I went in the bathroom, I'd keep my head down so I wouldn't have to look at myself. I stopped taking showers, because every time I got my head wet, more hair would fall out. Instead of washing my hair, I'd pour half a bottle of conditioner over it and set it in big sponge rollers to give it more body.

Before the press conference I had done the special "hat trick" I had developed to keep up the illusion that I

I held my very first press conference not as a Broadway star but as a leukemia patient soon after I left Memorial. There was one secret about my ordeal that I kept under my hat: My hair had thinned out so much as a result of chemotherapy and radiation that only a few wisps were left. For the press conference, I combed the remaining strands forward and popped a beret on my head to give the illusion of a headful of red hair. The reporters were none the wiser. © *by Harry Hamburg*

still had a full head of hair. I combed all the long stringy wisps forward to make bangs, and then I put on my beret to hold the hairdo in place. The fringe of hair that ringed my face made it look like I had a whole head of red hair. My gimmick was so effective that one newspaper later described me as "sporting a perky beret on my red hair."

I must have done something right, because after the press conference the radio and TV stations were buzzing with news of my recovery. "Little Shelley Bruce just came out of the hospital," reported one radio station, "and her prognosis is good."

It was so good that a month later my hair started growing back, and just three months later I found myself preparing to get up on stage again. The Kennedy Center was putting on a special televised show called "Broadway Plays Washington," as a benefit for public television. Stars from all the major Broadway shows would be there, doing numbers from their hits. Incredibly, I would be one of them! The *Annie* segment would feature me along with two other former Annies—Andrea and Sarah Jessica Parker, and the current star of the show, Allison Smith.

I had to pinch myself to believe it was true. Just a few months earlier, I had thought I would never be able to sing again. But now, I was going back to the Kennedy Center—the very place where I had taken my first steps to Broadway as an orphan five years before. Those few weeks of *Annie* previews in Washington had ushered in two exhilarating years of glamour and excitement on Broadway. Maybe this one night with the stars at Kennedy Center would begin a whole new life for me.

Maybe

But I didn't have time to sit around wondering. I pushed the daydreams aside and threw all my efforts into what I had to do to get ready for the show. No matter how much energy it took and no matter how hard I had to push myself, I was going to put everything I could into my one song, "Maybe."

It was the song Annie sang when the show opened, and it expressed the yearnings and longings deep inside her for the return of her real parents. "Maybe now its time, and maybe when I wake, they'll be there calling me ba-by—may-be," sang Annie.

In a strange way, the song summed up my yearnings and longings too. Maybe now it was time for me.

Maybe.

Tomorrow
Is Today

I knew something was different the minute the first notes were out of my mouth.

I was onstage rehearsing for "Broadway Plays Washington," and as I started to sing, I could feel my whole body shaking inside.

But something else was different—something too marvelous to imagine. My voice had changed, and somehow the notes were coming more easily. As I reached to hit one of the difficult high notes in "Maybe," I went for it—and it was *there*. For some inexplicable reason, I could hit the high notes more effortlessly than ever before. Impossible as it seemed, my range had actually *expanded*.

Anything Seems Possible

"Maybe it's a fluke," I thought. But when I sang the song again, the notes came just as they had before, rich and full with a dimension I never knew I possessed. Not

At sweet sixteen, without a care in the world, I'm singing "Tomorrow" at an awards dinner for the School of Visual Arts in New York City. I didn't know then that just five months later, in October 1981, I'd be a patient in Memorial Sloan-Kettering Cancer Center, wondering whether my singing career—and perhaps my life—would be over. Frank Tabaranza

only could I hit the high notes of the song, but I could actually go higher and higher.

I was shocked. My mother had heard it too. As she listened to me rehearse, she knew my voice had changed. She knew, too, that she had just witnessed a miracle. She confessed that after I came out of the hospital, she was sure my career was over and that I'd never be on stage again. She reasoned that a lot of people who might have wanted to hire me would hold back because I was sick. But now, all that had changed, and *anything* was possible.

On stage at the Kennedy Center's Opera House on the night of the show, I sang as never before. Just being in the show and working again made me feel terrific. In my bone-colored evening gown, I didn't look anything like the little Annie of Broadway. I was someone else. I was Shelley Bruce, the young woman who had licked cancer and was shouting it from the housetops.

Tapering Off

I'll have to admit that there were days afterward when I didn't feel like shouting—or singing. I was going to the hospital once a month for treatment with Dr. Murphy, and afterward I would take the drug prednisone at home for five days. While I was on the drug, I felt miserable. My emotions were out of control, and my moods would swing radically. One minute I'd be angry and hostile toward everyone; the next I'd dissolve in tears of depression. I hated myself during those periods. I felt like my life was a failure, and I wished I could just crawl into a hole and escape for a few days until it was time to taper myself off the drug.

But the worst ordeal came afterward, as I was coming off the medication. My back would go into terrible, agonizing muscle spasms, and my body would ache all over. I'd be walking and my knees would get so weak they'd almost buckle under me. During those periods I'd try to carry on a normal routine; but sometimes it was impossible, and I'd have to cancel my tutors or an appointment I had.

One time, during a particularly difficult bout, I wrote a poem to try to explain how I was feeling:

This medication makes me crazy,
It turns me upside down,
I think one minute I'm happy
Then a second later I frown.

Suddenly the tears begin
Again, I've lost control,
And all I feel I want to do
Is crawl into a hole.

Then quicker than quicksilver,
I'm changing moods again.
It happens so darn quickly,
And I never know just when.

It gets me really angry
When remarks come spewing out.
They seem to come from nowhere,
And start a major bout.

But the times I fear the most
Are the ones when I'm depressed;
I feel as if my life has been
A failure at its best.

But nothing's worse than near the end,
With all the aches and pains,
When even such a simple task
Can cause a heavy strain.

My back begins to gently pulse
And then it squeezes tight,

And suddenly I realize
I have no strength to fight.

And then I stand to go somewhere,
And unexpectedly I feel
As if I cannot walk at all,
The pain is just unreal.

My knees they feel so fragile,
As if about to break,
I fight to keep my eyes dry
Another step I cannot take.

For three days every month,
This goes on most every hour;
It drains me of all self-control
And every ounce of power.

But nothing can be done;
No pill to help the pain.
This is something I must endure;
It's a rule of this rotten game.

Living with leukemia *was* a rotten game. But, I was alive and singing, and that was worth holding on to. Most of the time I tried my best to keep on going as though nothing were wrong with me. It was either that or give up, and I wasn't about to do that. I had too many positive things in my life to abandon myself to bodily aches, pains, and weakness. I *had* to push on—just as I had pushed on with *Annie* day after day, and just as I had persevered through my hospitalization. I knew that if I let myself go, even just a little bit, it would become a habit, and I'd go deeper and deeper into a hole.

So, I went about my life, doing whatever I could to

make each day worthwhile. At times, when I felt like I couldn't walk a foot, I'd struggle to walk down the stairs of our house to visit my grandparents in the apartment below. At least that was accomplishing *something*, I'd tell myself. It was reassuring, too, to know that Dr. Murphy was just a phone call away. Any time of the day or night she'd call back within minutes with advice and words of support.

A New Breath of Life

The rest of the month, I felt a lot like my old self, and I'd fill the time with afternoon tutoring sessions and helping my mom run the children's talent agency she had just started. Often, I'd be called by agents who wanted me to audition for this or that, but I found myself becoming very selective about what I'd get involved with. I didn't jump at every chance that came along, because now my life was too important to me to simply run back and forth keeping busy for its own sake. If a role or a commercial came along that stimulated me, I'd try it. But I no longer wanted to keep hurtling through life at breakneck speed as I had in the past.

Somehow I had been given a new breath of life—a new beginning—and I wanted to make it count for something special. I had felt that new life come from deep within me on that rehearsal stage as I sang "Maybe" with new power and vitality. Not long after, on Easter eve, I understood the very source of that power.

I was sitting in St. Mary's Roman Catholic Church in Rutherford, New Jersey, during an Easter vigil, an ancient ritual that anticipates the resurrection of Christ on Easter morning. Next to me were my mother, grandmother, aunt, and cousins, and we had come, as we had every year, to share in quiet moments of reflection.

Not one to cool my heels, I appeared with former "orphan" Robyn Finn in the Goodspeed Opera House production of A Long Way to Boston *soon after leaving* **Annie.** *Wilson H. Brownell*

The service began in total darkness. Nothing stirred and nothing could be seen, except a few dim outlines in front of me. In the back of the church, the "Easter fire" had been lit in in a brazier, to symbolize the rekindling of the promise of Jesus. From that fire, the priest was lighting the giant Paschal candle, representing Christ, the "light of the world."

"Christ the light," intoned the priest.

"Thanks be to God," we responded.

Ever so slowly, he walked down the aisle, carrying the six-foot-long Paschal candle and touching it to the small candles we each held in our hands. Little by little, as the Paschal candle moved down the aisle toward the altar, the darkness began to lift.

"Christ the light," said the priest again.

"Thanks be to God," we responded.

From that one candle, the light spread throughout the congregation, until, suddenly, the church was ablaze with light.

"Christ the light," said the priest.

Thanks be to God," we responded.

The priest placed the Paschal candle on the altar, where it would burn for an entire year, and as he moved through the ritual, I began to sense that this light—lit from the Easter fire—was somehow meant especially for me. There was a promise there in the power of one light to overcome the darkness—a promise of hope to those without light and joy in their lives.

Although at that moment I couldn't figure out what it all meant, I could feel myself responding inside to the warm glow of the candlelight on the faces around me and to the images and messages of the service.

The priest continued the vigil by blessing the Easter water—a sign of baptism—that had washed away our sins and given us a fresh start in life. The same water would be used throughout the year for infant baptisms and for special blessings. But now, with Good Friday behind us and Easter a day away, the water was also a symbol of something much more immediate: It represented a rebaptism of sorts, through the crucifixion of Christ, into a new life of commitment.

Moments later, I found myself standing with the congregation to renew our baptismal vows. Sixteen years earlier, at my baptism, those words had been said for me by my godparents. Now, I was repeating them myself, as I had many times in the past, but this time there was a new urgency in my voice. It wasn't the words of the vow that touched me. It was the moment itself.

Just a few months earlier, I had been lying in a cancer hospital, stricken with leukemia. But there I was, at the Easter vigil, fully in remission and with a singing voice that was stronger than it had ever been before. It was as though I had started life all over again. I had been baptized into a whole new beginning, a whole new career, a whole new day.

I looked over at my mom and saw her eyes brimming with tears. She had felt it too.

As we left the church, she whispered to me, "I have my daughter again." Burning at the altar behind us was the Paschal candle.

An Echo of Easter

But another light had gone out. Little Yolanda, my first roommate at Memorial who had fought so hard to live, had died on Good Friday, just a few months before her second birthday.

At first, I didn't know what to do about the funeral, which was set for the following Monday. "Do you think I should go?" I asked my mother.

"I can't tell you that, Shelley," she said.

Finally, I knew I had to go. Yolanda and I had been so close, lying side by side in that hospital room. I almost felt like part of her family. I couldn't stay home, no matter how painful it was.

But there was more joy than pain that day. The service was filled with love and tenderness. One person read aloud all the cards and notes that had been sent to Yolanda's mother, and each one spoke of the happiness the little girl had given and the lives she had touched.

I think I might have gotten through the funeral without crying if I hadn't heard a baby cry. But as soon as I heard it, I imagined myself as a mother, facing what Yolanda's mother had just faced. To hear another baby cry at your own baby's funeral—I don't think I could have handled it. I started to cry, thinking about what it all meant.

I had been in the same room with Yolanda, I thought. And here I am, alive.

But then, Yolanda's mother began to speak. Her poignant testimony seemed to echo the Easter vigil that had touched me so deeply, and as I listened to her words, I began to understand what my own life could mean to others.

"I know she died for a reason," she said. "God saw that the climb up the mountain was getting too hard. But Yolanda is carrying her light into a different room. We can't see her, but we can tell where she's been by the little lights she has left behind."

Back to Broadway

In the days and weeks afterward, I felt a new sense of purpose. No matter how hard my physical struggle was, every day was a new opportunity to make the world a little brighter. That's why I was here. That's what I had been prepared for as Annie. And as long as my light was shining, I would try make it something terrific!

It wasn't long before I was given the chance to put myself to the test. One day I received a call from Walter Willison, a producer who along with Jefrey Silverman was putting together a cabaret show based loosely on the life of Ruby Keeler. He had seen me on television in "Broadway Plays Washington," he said, and wanted me to audition for the role of "Sandy McGuire," which was fashioned after Ruby Keeler.

I put on my best red wig, sveltest black leotard and tights, and "kickiest" high-heeled tap shoes and sang and danced my way into the part.

The show was *Broadway Scandals of 1928*, which ran during the summer at O'Neal's Times Square. The setting was Texas Guinan's New York speakeasy, and the story revolved around the wedding day of her star performer, Sandy McGuire. In real life, Ruby had fallen in love with a gangster whom she had jilted for Al Jolson after she ran off to Hollywood and took the town by storm. But in the play, Sandy came back and married the gangster instead.

I was thrilled to be part of the Broadway scene again and even more excited that I could handle the demands. Even though the pace was grueling, somehow it only inspired me to work harder. The show ran four evenings a week and twice on Friday and Saturday evenings, which meant we barely had time to turn around before going back on again. But I didn't mind. I was doing what I loved, and I was managing to come through even during those tough moments when I was on medication.

What's more, I was doing it as *me!* When the show started, I took off my wig, and in my short, curly hair I looked just like the 1920's "flapper" I was supposed to be.

I felt very grown-up in the role and even more so

because I got my first stage kiss from actor Kenny D'Aquila, who played the gangster. At first, though, the idea of being kissed onstage bothered me, and I said "No, no, I don't think this is going to work." Then I figured, "Well, it's part of the job." And then, I said, "Well, it's not so bad!"

The thing that meant the most to me, though, was how happy the show made Ruby Keeler. She came on opening night, not only because the play was based on her life, but also because her daughter-in-law, Gwen Hillier Lowe, was in the cast. After the show was over, she came up to me and said, "I couldn't think of anyone better to play me!" As we sat and talked, in a nostalgic moment she confessed that she liked the ending of the play because in her heart she had always wanted to marry the gangster!

What I loved about her was her gentleness. She was such a warm, happy person, and I was glad she had seen a little of that in me. I felt like the sparkle had come back into my life, and more than anything else, I wanted to pass it on.

Even after the show closed, I was still carried away with enthusiasm. *Broadway Scandals* had shown me that my career, far from being over, was just beginning. Stretched out ahead of me could be many wonderful years of performing. The important thing was to take each opportunity as it came and give it my best shot for that moment—and everything else would fall into place.

And it did. A few months after *Broadway Scandals* closed, I fulfilled a dream that probably belongs to every kid who has ever watched the Macy's Thanksgiving Day Parade. Thanks to advertising executive Emily Whelan, I was asked to ride the "Doodle Bug" float and sing "On a Wonderful Day Like Today," in the 1982 parade.

Ever since I was a little girl, I had gone to the parade. I had stood along Broadway waving at the floats and

Less than a year after my hospitalization for leukemia, I was back on stage in Broadway Scandals of 1928, where I played a "flapper" fashioned after actress Ruby Keeler.
© *1982 by Susan Cook*

dreaming that someday I'd have the chance to ride on one too.

Suddenly, there I was, up on top of the doodle bug—a comical creature with a long, wavy body that zig-zagged down Broadway. It was a very bumpy ride! There seemed to be an awful lot of potholes in the road, and without anything to hold onto, I felt as though I were going to fall off at any minute.

But there was too much going on around me to worry too much about safety. The streets were thick with people, all smiling and happy despite the brisk November weather. There were people on every side of me, and high above in the office buildings, thousands more peered out of windows and waved. I felt like the heroine of some great adventure—being cheered and applauded by the crowds. What made the experience so much fun was that the float moved slowly enough for me to talk to people as I rode by.

"It's cold down here," someone would shout. And I'd smile back and say, "I'm freezing here too!" Even my white curly lamb jacket couldn't quite take the edge off the cold.

But as soon as we hit Herald Square, right in front of Macy's where the TV cameras were stationed, I could feel myself warming up. And in front of millions of eyes all across America, I sang, "On a Wonderful Day Like Today."

That Thanksgiving Day *was* wonderful. I thought about how only a year before I had spent Thanksgiving with my family inside Memorial Hospital. And yet, there I was, standing in front of Herald Square and belting out a song that summed up my joy in having another day to be alive and sing about.

The Benefit Circuit

During the next few months I became a sought-after speaker on the benefit circuit—mostly benefits for the American Cancer Society. I hopped around the country, speaking and singing before groups of volunteers who supported the Cancer Society's work.

Everywhere I went I talked about my experience in the hospital and explained how I was living with leukemia. And always, as I had when I played Annie, I would sing "Tomorrow."

Then one day I got the exciting news that I would be going to the White House again, not as Annie, but as myself. I had been named to receive the American Cancer Society's National Cancer Courage Award. As honorary chairperson of the Society, First Lady Nancy Reagan would be making the presentation. I had met Mrs. Reagan just a few months before I sang at a U.S.O. luncheon honoring her.

My parents and grandparents trouped to Washington for the occasion, which was set for four o'clock March 25, 1983. The only thing to mar the day was that Grandma almost didn't get through the East Gate of the White House! She had brought her birth certificate for identification and, of course, it had her maiden name on it. Since her married name was on the list of approved guests, the guard at the gate wouldn't let her through. But, finally, the tangle was cleared up, and we enjoyed a personal tour of the White House given by a Secret Service agent. Then we all moved to the second floor for the ceremonies.

Living a Role

So much had happened since I had been at the White House nearly six years before as an *Annie* orphan, doing

My hand holds a handkerchief still wet with tears, along with an award from the American Cancer Society presented to me by First Lady Nancy Reagan. "I never expected to cry," I told Mrs. Reagan at the White House ceremony on March 25, 1983.

As I greet Mrs. Reagan at the American Cancer Society award presentations, my dad, Bruce Merklinghaus, follows behind on the receiving line. Dad was the inspiration for my stage name, "Shelley Bruce." The White House

cartwheels down the hall with Amy Carter. The White House had changed; I had changed; and nothing would be the same again.

But somehow that day at the White House was much more special than my first visit. Then, I had been one of the gang of orphans who had taken Washington by storm. This time, though, I had come to the White House as a different kind of celebrity—one who hadn't just played a role but had *lived* it, just as many others less famous had done before me.

The ceremony was short and sweet. Dr. Willis J. Taylor, president of the American Cancer Society introduced Mrs. Reagan to present the award. In a quiet voice, she said she wanted to read the inscription because she thought everyone would like to hear it. Then she read aloud "The American Cancer Society salutes Shelley Bruce for her personal courage in her battle against cancer and for the hope and inspiration she gives all Americans in the fight for life and health."

"Congratulations," she said.

I stood up and said a few words of thanks, but as I started to thank my family, the tears just started coming.

"I never expected to cry," I told the guests. I struggled to get out a few more words. "I'd like to thank my family," I said.

That's all I could get out. The tears kept coming. They were running down my face and dripping all over my brand-new silk suit and red and white silk blouse, and there was nothing I could do about it. I just stood there and cried.

As Dr. Taylor jumped in with some closing remarks, Mrs. Reagan put her arm around me and held me tight.

I don't know what came over me. As Annie I had learned to turn the tears on and off on cue. But this time, they were out of control. For the first time, the enormity of all that I had been through during the preceding year and a half finally came home to me. What got me were the words of the inscription: " . . . the hope and inspiration she gives . . . "

Was that really *me* she was talking about? A few days later, I understood how the words on the award applied to me when I received a letter from a college student who had just seen one of the road productions of *Annie* in Westbury, New York, and was moved to write. The letter was dated April 3, 1983—Easter Sunday:

An Answered Prayer

Dear Shelley:

I saw Annie last Friday night, April 1, at Westbury Music Fair. I couldn't wait to see it even though I had already seen it on Broadway. It's my favorite show because it champions the goodness in people and the good that we are all capable of doing for one another.

Yesterday, while I was thinking about the play, I started to think of you and your fight against illness. Now, I have never been a person with very strong religious convictions. It has always been difficult for me to put much faith in religion when I looked around and saw the tremendous amount of human suffering that abounds in our world today.

So you can imagine how strange I felt when an urgent need to pray suddenly swept over me while I was thinking of you. It was a feeling that I have never experienced before, and yet, at the same time, it was the most natural feeling in the world. And so, after thinking about what I should say, I fell to my knees and began to pray in earnest for you. It was a very emotional moment for me, and I started to cry almost uncontrollably. But I managed to finish my prayer. That strong sense of purpose and emotion never left me for the rest of the day.

This morning as I went downstairs to breakfast, I stopped to read the Sunday paper. My heart nearly skipped a beat as I turned the page and looked down to see an article telling about your wonderful recovery. It had been less than twenty-four hours since I had said my prayer, and here was what I had asked for looking at me from the page. It may have been nothing more than coincidence, but inside I know that it was more than that. I felt as if God was telling me in his own way that you were doing well.

I cannot describe the joy and happiness I felt at that moment. I just had to believe that God was watching over you. That was the best Easter gift that I could receive.

Shelley, I don't know what your religious beliefs are, but believe me when I say that mine will never be the same. I will never look at things the same again. I have never met you, but after today's experience, I feel as if you are my best friend. This all may sound strange, but I can't explain it to myself any better than I already have to you.

All my best wishes.

· As I read his letter, which was so open and honest with emotion, my hand trembled with joy. I thought about the millions of people like this sensitive student, who are just waiting for a sign of hope to give their own lives purpose. And I realized that in some cases, my own experience might even be a means to reach out and touch them.

Even though it isn't always easy living with leukemia, I'm alive and singing—and that's worth shouting about. Before a crowd of 800 volunteers of the American Cancer Society in Atlanta in January 1983, I belted out a medley of hits, including, of course, "Tomorrow."

All My Tomorrows

All I had tried to do, really, was keep my own life going by keeping myself singing. That's what Annie had done, too, when she sang "Tomorrow" before a roomful of cabinet members in FDR's White House and inspired the New Deal. As she gave them new hope for the future, she was giving herself a dose of positive thinking, as well.

But in my own *real* life, I've learned something that Annie never knew: I don't have to wait until tomorrow to find out what life has in store for me. What happens tomorrow depends on what I do right now. If I do the best I can in every present moment, then the sun will surely come out—not only tomorrow, but today as well.

Sporting a red wig after my hospitalization, I'm back at home with my beloved cat, Fidi, and poodle, Babette. Mary McLoughlin—N.Y. Post

Annie:
An Introduction to
the Cast and
Creators

When *Annie* closed on Broadway on January 2, 1983, after 2,377 performances, there wasn't a dry eye in the Uris Theater, except maybe Sandy's.

As the final curtain came down that night, I was standing off to the side of the orchestra, waiting for Martin Charnin to call me up to the stage in what would be my final bow as an Annie, albeit a former one. All through the show that night, I had watched misty-eyed from the audience as the last Annie, Alyson Kirk, said the lines that had once been mine. Everything about her Annie was different—she had another Daddy Warbucks (Harve Presnell), another mean Miss Hannigan (June Havoc), and another slant on the character of Annie, which I had tried to play with a mixture of toughness and tenderness. Then there were the orphans, who almost seemed too young to be in the roles—I guess that was a sign of my own advancing age!

But not much had really changed about *Annie*. It was just that I was getting older—nearly eighteen to be exact. In my black leather pants, black and white cowgirl boots, and red and white silk blouse, I was hardly the "entrancing moppet" I had been on opening night in 1977 as the orphan Kate. Nor was I the little girl with the big voice who had starred as Annie in 1978.

It was hard to believe that nearly six years had passed since *Annie* had opened on Broadway. In those six years, *Annie* had become an institution. It was the seventh longest running musical on Broadway, behind *Grease*, *Fiddler on the Roof*, *A Chorus Line*, *Hello, Dolly!*, *My Fair Lady*, and *Oh Calcutta!* It had won twenty-two major theater awards, including:

- Seven Tony Awards
- A New York Drama Critics' Circle Award for best musical
- Seven Drama Desk Awards
- Five Outer Critics' Circle Awards
- A *Theater World* Award
- A Grammy for its cast album
- *Cue* magazine's Golden Apple Award

At its height of popularity, the show had had four touring companies throughout the United States playing simultaneously along with the Broadway production. Each national company was as carefully selected and trained as the original, and to make the shows fresh and exciting, new dialogue and original musical numbers were added for each company. Around the world, *Annie* had been seen by an estimated twenty million people and had been translated into twenty-one languages. It had been performed by twenty-seven foreign companies in England, Denmark, Sweden, Norway, Finland, Holland,

Japan, Australia, South Africa, Venezuela, New Zealand, West Germany, Ireland, the Philippines, Spain, Greece, Argentina, and Mexico, where *Annie* is known as *Anita*.

Over the years, about 12,000 girls—and even one boy—had auditioned for the roles of Annie and the other orphans. The boy had shown up for an open call, saying that he couldn't understand why males couldn't be in the orphanage, too. The casting director explained that the sexes were segregated back in the thirties, and so for the sake of accuracy, no boys could be cast in the show.

Financially, the show was a blockbuster, grossing more than $225 million—including a $9.5 million sale to Columbia Pictures that was the most money ever paid for the rights to a stage production or novel. The estimated $20 million in profits has made key people like Martin Charnin, Thomas Meehan, Charles Strouse, Peter Gennaro, and some of the producers wealthy.

Martin, who was $75,000 in debt before the show opened, likes to say that "Everybody has already made enough money off it to last the rest of their natural lives."

The show was around so long that during its run ticket prices nearly tripled. When the show opened at the Goodspeed Opera House, the best seat in the house went for $12. On Broadway, the initial tab for a Saturday night orchestra seat was $17.50, but by the time *Annie* closed, the same seat had jumped to $35.

Despite its success, by the fall of 1982 the show was beginning to lose $30,000 to $40,000 a week, primarily because the *Annie* road companies were such a hit. That was Martin's explanation at any rate. "Visitors weren't coming to see *Annie* anymore," he said, "because they had already seen it in Memphis or Peoria."

So, as the New Year opened in 1983, I stood in the Uris Theater awaiting my cue in the grand finale of *Annie*. The curtain had come down, the last Broadway cast had taken their bows, and Martin was up on stage introducing everyone who had anything to do with the show. Only five members of the original cast were still with the show: Raymond Thorne, who played FDR; Dick Ensslen, an ensemble member who played a variety of roles; Edwin Bordo, who was Daddy Warbucks' butler, Drake; Don Bonell, a member of the ensemble; and the one and only Sandy, who played himself.

By the time Martin got to me and the other Annies, the stage was packed with hundreds of people—producers, former cast members and crew—who had come to share one last moment of glory. There were a string of Daddy Warbucks, a bevy of Miss Hannigans, and close to 150 orphans drawn from the road companies and Broadway.

My eyes scanned the crowd on the stage in front of me, and as I spotted the familiar faces of those I had worked with so closely, I found myself choking up with emotion. On one side of the stage were the original orphans—Donna Graham, Danielle Brisebois, Janine Ruane, Robyn Finn, and Diana Barrows. On the other side were Sandy Faison, who had played Miss Farrell, and Laurie Beechman, whose fabulous voice had turned her small part of A Star to Be into a sensation.

Just seeing them—and remembering—brought tears to my eyes.

But Martin's voice made me snap back into my role as a star because he had begun to reel off the names of the four former Annies in reverse order. Up to the stage ran Allison Smith, who had started as the youngest Annie and ended up as the longest running of all of us. After her came Sarah Jessica Parker, who had succeeded me, and then, I heard my name being called.

I raced up on stage, my heart beating with excitement, as cheers of the audience carried me forward. By then, the applause was a steady hum that seemed to go on and on. I hugged Martin and stood at the front of the stage with the other Annies. Then, we watched expectantly as the three people who had made *Annie* an overnight smash—Andrea McArdle, Reid Shelton, and Dorothy Loudon—come up on stage.

The audience went wild. We all went wild.

Finally, in a last outpouring of sentiment, we all joined together in singing "Tomorrow." By the time the final notes were sung, the air in the Uris Theater was heavy with emotion. For a few moments we all stood transfixed in our places on stage. No one wanted to leave.

But just as the show itself was a finely tuned production, so was the grand finale of *Annie*, which was directed down to the last detail by Martin Charnin. On cue, we all moved offstage, leaving him sitting alone with the set of Daddy Warbucks' Christmas-bedecked mansion behind him.

In a moment of high drama, Martin ordered Drake, Daddy Warbucks' butler, to "close the house." With that, actor Edwin Bordo switched off the lights on the Christmas tree. Seconds later he cut the stage lights, leaving the theater in total darkness. All that could be seen was a faint flurry of artificial snow, which had started to fall gently on stage.

Everything was quiet. Suddenly, the stillness was broken by Martin, who called writer Thomas Meehan to the stage. "Listen, I've got an idea," said Martin. "What would you think if . . . " Then he whispered something in Tom's ear.

Tom looked up and smiled. "Annie," he said, and then he held up two fingers on his right hand. With that, *Annie, Part II* was on its way.

A final cheer went up from the audience, and then, *Annie* was no more.

Today, the sequel is already in the works, and there are plans to revive the original show every year at Christmas as an annual event like *The Nutcracker*. But whatever the future holds for new versions of the show, *Annie* will always have special meaning for the millions who saw it and the hundreds who performed in it.

For many of those I worked with, there was a pot of gold at the end of the *Annie* rainbow. Some people literally became rich because of it. Others, like Dorothy Loudon, became famous. Still others found that their brush with greatness opened doors to new careers and to even more challenging personal adventures.

Now, as my own kind of "grand finale," I want to invite you to take a closer look at this Broadway family of mine—the actors and creators of the show with whom I shared a special bond and whose tomorrows will be shaped by *Annie* forever.

CAST OF CHARACTERS

Publisher's Note: The following list of characters includes those actors and actresses who were part of the original Broadway cast. During the entire run of the production, there were four other Annies, in addition to Shelley. Also, of the original orphans, only four remained when Shelley became Annie: Diana Barrows, Danielle Brisebois, Robyn Finn, and Donna Graham. Two new ones—Kim Fedena, and Sarah Jessica Parker—stepped in to replace Janine Ruane, and Shelley, and soon after, Jennine Babo took over from Danielle Brisebois.

THE ANNIES

ANNIE #1: *ANDREA McARDLE*

When Andrea jumped onstage at the Broadway opening of Annie on April 21, 1977, she simply wowed the critics. At thirteen, she was declared "perfect" for the role. In every respect, she claimed the hearts of audiences who literally wanted to wrap her up and take her home.

Sandy upstages five of his favorite ladies (clockwise from lower left): Annie #4, Allison Smith; #3, Sarah Jessica Parker; #1, Andrea McArdle; #2, me; and #5, Alyson Kirk. Dan Brinzac—N.Y. Post

For her portrayal of Annie as a tough and streetwise kid, she became the youngest performer ever to win a Tony Award nomination for best actress in a Broadway musical.

Andrea's triumphant opening at the Alvin may have marked her debut on Broadway, but she was by no means a novice. She had been performing since the age of three in her hometown, Philadelphia, after an agent spotted her in a fifty-cents-a-week dance class and suggested she do commercials. By the time she was eight, she had decided that acting was a great way to get out of school! Thirty-five television commercials later and after dinner theater stints with the *King and I* and *The Sound of Music*, Andrea won a part in the CBS soap opera, *Search for Tomorrow*. For her outstanding performance as Wendy Wilkins on that show, Andrea won the 1976 award for best juvenile actress on afternoon TV. She stayed in the role for two and a half years.

Andrea attributes her success to her training in Philadelphia. "There are a lot of places you can sing in Philadelphia, like the U.S.O. variety shows," she told a reporter from the *New Yorker*. "In New York, you only get a chance to audition, but in Philadelphia, instead of an audition, you wind up with a part in a small show. In New York, until you make it big, you don't really make it at all."

Well, Andrea "made it," of course, and after a year at the top as Annie on Broadway, she opened the show in London, where she played for eighty performances—the most allowed by England's child labor laws. Then it was back to Philadelphia—to high school, proms, athletics, and the normal teen routine. The experience, she says, was sobering.

"When I was in *Annie*," she explained to a *New York Times* reporter, "I'd go to Sardi's every night and see Paul

McCartney, Barbra Streisand, stars like that. There was no reality at all.

"When I went home, I'd call up my friends and say, 'Let's go to a movie,' and they'd say, 'We don't have any money,' and I'd say, 'Why not?' I found out you can't do whatever you want to do whenever you want to do it. I'd have lost a lot of friends if I hadn't learned that lesson."

But even though she was away from the glitter of Broadway, Andrea never really stopped working. She starred in *Rainbow,* an NBC television movie based on the story of the early life of Judy Garland. Also, she did charity benefits and a tour with Liberace, and she made three TV pilots and dozens of guest TV appearances with Johnny Carson, Merv Griffin, Dinah Shore, and Mike Douglas.

After graduating from high school in 1981, she returned to New York in a cabaret show, "They Say It's Wonderful," at the St. Regis-Sheraton. In the revue, a tribute to Irving Berlin, she was teamed with Larry Kert, Debbie Shapiro, and Terry Burrell. But a reviewer said it was Andrea's rendition of the title song that stole the show.

Since then, she's crisscrossed the country in regional productions of *Meet Me in St. Louis, The Fantastiks, Annie Get Your Gun, Grease,* and *They're Playing Our Song.* These days she's in New York to study acting and, of course, to keep on working.

Andrea's come a long way from the days when she rode her skateboard down Shubert Alley as an adolescent on Broadway. As for the time she put the "green slime" on her hand during the scene with FDR's cabinet, she admits that she got a kick out of seeing the other actors' faces when they shook her hand. "I thought that was hilarious," she says. "Now I don't think it's so funny."

Her attitude about critics has changed, too. "Before, if

someone had said, 'Do a good job, so-and-so is in the audience,' I'd say, 'Oh, boy!' like a friend was coming to see the show." But now, she says, she gets nervous because, "I'm just more aware."

But perhaps the biggest lesson she's learned from *Annie* and the aftermath of her success is that she knows what it takes to be a professional. "I'm not a star, and I don't think I ever was," says Andrea. "If you think [you were a star], you can get hung up when you're not." She says of her year as Annie, "I was a working actress then, and I'm a working actress now. That's how I like to think of it."

ANNIE #2: *SARAH JESSICA PARKER*

"When it's time to go, it'll be very sad," Sarah Jessica once said of the inevitable end of her year as Annie, which she played from 1979 to 1980. "But you can't be Annie forever. It'd be abnormal."

But there was nothing at all abnormal about Sarah Jessica's aspirations for the stage. She's the fourth of eight kids in a very active theater family, headed by her father, Hal, an actor and stage manager, and her mother, Barbara Forste, a teacher. Before she rose to fame in *Annie*, Sarah and four of her siblings toured with Shirley Jones in *The Sound of Music*, and four of them toured in the same show with Sally Ann Howes. At the time she starred in *Annie*, her younger sister, Megan, was appearing in *Evita*, and another sibling was on the boards in an Equity Library Theater production off Broadway.

Sarah brought to *Annie* a wealth of acting and dancing credits from off Broadway, films, television, radio, and even ballet. She had acted in the off Broadway production of *By Strouse* at the Manhattan Theater Club and had danced professionally in *La Sylphide* with the American Ballet Theatre and in *The Firebird* and *The Nutcracker* for the Cincinnati Ballet Company.

Her move to Broadway from her hometown, Cincinnati, came at age eleven, when she answered an ad and landed the role of Flora in the Broadway revival of Harold Pinter's *The Innocents* with Claire Bloom. The short-lived show was memorable, she says, because between shows Bloom invited her back to her apartment to nap and would give her motherly advice. "She'd do things like making me eat an orange every day," says Sarah.

Two years later, Sarah Jessica found herself back on Broadway as the orphan July in *Annie*. When she was tapped for the lead in 1979, the fourteen-year-old actress had already played the title role twelve times as an understudy—five with Dorothy Loudon and seven with Alice Ghostley as Miss Hannigan.

"I was the oldest Annie they'd ever had," Sarah says, "and I grew five inches during the year I had the part." She also was the first Annie to commute to New York every day with the show's canine star Sandy, who lived in a neighboring town in New Jersey. The two grew so close that sometimes she'd dogsit for him on weekends.

From the moment she became Annie, Sarah has had her eyes firmly fixed on her own tomorrows. "I dream about getting a Tony, although I'd have to do a new play to win one," she told the *New York Times* when she took over the Annie role. "And I'd like to dance with Baryshnikov. I dream about that, too. He's so neat."

Since *Annie*, Sarah hasn't wasted a minute in pursuing her dreams of stardom:

She's made movies, most recently *Footloose*, done in 1983 with John Lithgow, Kevin Bacon, Lori Singer, and Chris Penn.

She's appeared with the Metropolitan Opera in its productions of *Hansel and Gretel, Pagliacci, Cavalleria Rusticana, L'Enfant et les Sortileges,* and *Le Rossignol.*

She's been featured on a number of television specials including ABC's "My Body, My Child" with Vanessa Redgrave; "Do Me a Favor . . . Don't Vote for My Mom" with Kelly Reno and Dina Merrill.

And she worked in two soap operas, *Another World* and *Capitol.*

But her biggest triumph yet is in the CBS situation comedy series *Square Pegs,* in which she plays a not-so-popular California high school freshman named Patty Greene, who want to run with the "in" crowd of Valley Girls.

As Patty, says Sarah, "My clothes are not particularly appealing and I wear just enough makeup to make me look alive—nothing more. I wear the wrong shape glasses, I slouch. You think of a TV series as being glamourous, with thousands of people working to make you look beautiful. Well, it's not always true."

But no matter how she's supposed to appear as Patty, Sarah's own star is shining brightly. As one of the story editors of *Square Pegs* told *TV Guide,* Sarah has a "wonderful, exciting future . . . We've only scratched the surface of what she's going to deliver."

ANNIE #3: *ALLISON SMITH*

It was a Cinderella story come true: A little girl from New Jersey, who had never been on a stage in her life—not even for a school play—answered an ad to try out for *Annie* and walked away with the title role. To get it, she had outsung and outacted 500 other girls who had showed up at the Alvin Theater for an open call.

Just like that, Allison Smith was a Broadway star.

When she took over the role in January, 1980, just one month past her tenth birthday, she was the youngest Annie ever. But she also stayed with the role longer than any other Annie—for two and a half years in 1,056 performances.

Even at age ten, she was a quick study on stage. Just six months into the show, for example, she was in the middle of singing "Tomorrow" when Sandy, the dog, threw up right in front of her. Here's how she described the scene in *Interview* magazine:

"I was supposed to tell Sandy to sit down, and he wouldn't. He just kept on bouncing up and down and then he started throwing up—these three big piles. He was stepping in it and everything, and he stood right in front of me doing it."

Luckily, said Allison, the next scene was "Hooverville"—when Annie comes upon some down- and-outers living in a shantytown under the Fifty-ninth Street Bridge. "The Hoovervillites came on stage and they started wiping up the mess and they gave it to one of the stagehands," she said. "The audience really cracked up when one of the Hoovervillites asked me, 'Hey kid, ya hungry?' and I said, 'No, but my dog is!' "

With that retort, Allison marked herself a real pro, and in the years since she's had lots of opportunities to demonstrate her versatility and presence of mind as an actress. She's been a frequent star on television, appearing in network series such as *Silver Spoons* with Ricky Schroder and performing in a number of variety shows and specials with such stars as Rita Moreno, Joe Namath, Erik Estrada, Tony Randall, and Jerry Stiller.

She has also appeared on the Easter Seals Telethon and the Jerry Lewis Telethon, and she has been the Youth Chairperson for the Cystic Fibrosis Foundation.

ANNIE #4: *ALYSON KIRK*

Alyson is a girl made after Annie's gritty heart.

When she was sitting in the audience of *Annie* on her ninth birthday on January 14, 1979, watching none other than Shelley Bruce sing "Tomorrow," she decided right then and there to shoot for the stars.

"I'm going to be the next Annie," she told her mom.

Three years later, at the age of twelve, she made it. As the last Annie on Broadway, she only had four months in the role, and yet, it didn't really matter. What counted was that Alyson had reached her goal. She succeeded her friend and neighbor, Allison Smith, who was in the audience to cheer her at her opening.

Alyson joined the cast of *Annie* in June 1982, as the orphan Kate and was later named Allison's understudy. She's the only Annie to have toured in the show prior to coming to Broadway. From 1980 to 1981 she appeared as Kate in the third national company of *Annie*, and before moving to Broadway she did numerous commercials.

Since the show closed, she's appeared in a documentary film called *Growing Up on Broadway*.

THE ORPHANS

DIANA BARROWS (Tessie)

Now known as the "Oh my goodness!" orphan, for her portrayal of Annie's nervous friend with the pigtails, Diana started her professional career at the ripe old age of one by appearing in a diaper commercial. She has continued modeling and appearing in commercials, some of which, she says, can get kind of silly. In one, she recalls, "My mom is frying chicken and I had to run in screaming that my brother fell out of a tree. She runs out and when we come back two hours later with his arm in a cast, the chicken still isn't greasy!"

Despite these occasional thin plot lines, Diana loves performing, and prior to *Annie* she was seen on Broadway and at the Kennedy Center in Washington in the revival of *Cat on a Hot Tin Roof.* Diana also had a leading role in the off Broadway production of *Panama Hattie,* and played Amaryllis in a touring company of *The Music Man.*

In *Annie* she originated the role of Tessie at the Goodspeed Opera House and played the part for two years on Broadway.

The linguist among the orphans, Diana speaks three foreign languages—French, Spanish, and Portuguese—and since *Annie* she's been working on a fourth—Japanese. After leaving the show in June 1978, she went to Japan four times with a group called the New York Fire Crackers. The song-and-dance group, organized and created by Japanese composer Kei Ogura, has become known throughout Japan for their socially conscious musical productions, aimed at teenagers. In Japan, Diana has made TV guest appearances, commercials, and records.

Back home in New York, Diana graduated a year early from the Professional Children's School in Manhattan, and now she's a drama major at New York University. In her spare time she has sung at a benefit for James Cagney sponsored by the New York Press Club, done commercials, and appeared with Shelley in *Growing Up on Broadway,* an educational film produced by Johnson and Johnson about the joys and pains of growing up in show business.

"Everyone in *Annie* went up for the movie," Diana says. For today's children, she adds, "*Annie* kids are heroines."

DANIELLE BRISEBOIS (Molly)

Danielle's first spoken words as an infant weren't "Mama" or "Da-da" but "Sit down!" Maybe that's a clue to how she sometimes walked off with the show.

One New York reviewer (Alan Rich) said his heart was "stolen by this seven-year-old bundle of radiance." With her high-pitched wail and a flash of toothless smile, Danielle instantly endeared herself to audiences—a little moppet with a gigantic personality that simply dominated the stage.

Now a frequent star on TV's *Archie Bunker's Place*, Danielle was already a seasoned performer before she joined *Annie* at the Goodspeed Opera House. She has appeared on TV's *Kojak* and has appeared at the City Center in New York in *The Saint of Bleecker Street*. She also performed in the film *Mom, the Wolfman and Me*.

Danielle had done over fifty commercials and voice-overs by the time she joined the Broadway cast, and she was a widely used magazine model. Also, she was the youngest child to ever have her own nightclub act in New York City.

JANINE RUANE (July)

Janine had appeared in national touring productions of *The Sound of Music* and *Here's Love* before appearing in *Annie*. She had performed in *The King and I* at the Downingtown Inn Dinner Theatre and was also in the 1976 Milliken Breakfast Show.

ROBYN FINN (Pepper)

Some believe Pepper was the "toughest" orphan as the part was written in the script. But Robyn, who can speak with obvious authority because she actually played the role, believes Pepper was probably the least tough of all the girls—even if she was somewhat unruly. Robyn admits she enjoyed playing the part because, "I could never act that way in real life. On stage I can behave that way and know I won't have to suffer the consequences."

Robyn, who hails from Boston, was one of the new orphans in the cast when the show moved from Connecticut to Broadway. At fourteen, she was the oldest orphan and also the one with the least acting experience, although she had been singing professionally since the age of five.

But it wasn't the acting that was tough for Robyn—it was getting her shoulder-length hair cut into a curly bob for her role in *Annie*. "She cried for three days," said her mother. To make matters worse, her natural red hair looked too much like Annie's, so during the pre-Broadway run in Washington, it had to be dyed brown. "She cried for three more days," her mother added.

Following her stint in *Annie*, Robyn appeared with Shelley in *A Long Way to Boston* at the Goodspeed Opera House—with her hair back to its own bright red. Today, her face is familiar to television audiences who have seen her in national commercials.

DONNA GRAHAM (Duffy)

A newcomer to Broadway at age twelve, Donna had a wide professional background doing commercials and voice-overs. By the time she joined *Annie* as Duffy, she had already been a successful model as well as a recording artist with a group called the Exemptions.

A straight A student in school, Donna always impressed interviewers with her level-headed approach to her fame in *Annie*. Although she keeps high hopes for the future, she's aware of the fleeting nature of the spotlight. "On Broadway," she says, "you just never know."

A native of Philadelphia, Donna appeared in the 1976

Milliken Show and has sung at Atlantic City's Steel Pier and at a number of other clubs.

KIM FEDENA (Kate)

After her off Broadway debut in *By Strouse*, Kim went on immediately to debut on Broadway as Kate, following Shelley Bruce in *Annie*. When she joined the cast at age twelve, Kim already had a wealth of experience.

Well known on the supper-club circuit in the Pennsylvania and New Jersey area, Kim has also done benefits with Julia DeJohn in Philadelphia. She has appeared on television in *The New Mouseketeers* as well as in several commercials.

Kim, who began singing professionally at age four, first studied voice and dance in Philadelphia. Then, in New York, she studied drama with Lee Strasberg.

Since *Annie*, Kim has been concentrating on developing her voice, and she has put together a nightclub act featuring songs from Broadway shows. Charles Strouse, the man behind the *Annie* music, has been her musical director.

Her latest venture is a recording, "I Love the New York Yankees," which will be played during ballgames at Yankee Stadium.

JENNINE BABO (Molly)

As Molly, the youngest orphan, Jennine made her Broadway debut at the age of seven, taking over the role originated by Danielle Brisebois. Even then, she could count herself a show business veteran. A native of Philadelphia, Jennine got her start by singing and dancing in USO shows at Valley Forge and Fort Dix when she was only four. By the time she hit the stage in *Annie*, the seasoned young actress had already done a number of television commercials and voice-overs.

Jennine spent five years in *Annie* on Broadway in various orphan roles: first as Molly, then as Tessie, and finally as Duffy.

THE ORIGINAL BROADWAY CAST

DOROTHY LOUDON (Miss Hannigan)

This mean, wicked mistress of the orphanage mistreated her poor charges miserably—to the delight of thousands. With her sneering "Do I hear happiness in there?" Dorothy's brilliant performance made Miss Hannigan one of the great comic villains of Broadway.

"I tell you, this show is the most important thing that ever happened to me," Dorothy said at one point during the run. But she didn't want to do it at first. "There's an old saying, 'Never be in a show with kids, dogs, or an Irish tenor,' and this show had all three!"

As inspiration for her part, Dorothy said she had three sources: women reading the racing form on the subways; twenty-five "beastly" children with whom she worked in an industrial show; and her role as Beatrice in a national tour of Paul Zindel's Pulitzer Prize-winning *The Effect of Gamma Rays on Man-in-the-Moon Marigolds.*

Before *Annie*, Dorothy appeared in the off Broadway production of *The World of Jules Feiffer*, directed by Mike Nichols. Her performance in *Annie* earned her a Tony Award as best actress in a musical, as well as the Drama Desk and Outer Critics' Circle awards.

She debuted on Broadway in *Nowhere to Go But Up*, which, Dorothy recalled, was "the first show ever to be picketed by its backers, who wanted to close it down." Since then she has made award-winning appearances in *Three Men on a Horse*, *The Fig Leaves Are Falling*, and Noel Coward's *Sweet Potato*.

In her nightclub tours, Dorothy says, her act brought down the house—but not in the way you would expect: "They burned down! I've closed so many clubs that way . . . a club in Cleveland, a club in Montreal, a club in Troy, New York . . . I don't like to leave New York!"

Since *Annie*, Dorothy has starred on Broadway as Mrs. Lovett in *Sweeney Todd*, and she also appeared with Katharine Hepburn in *The West Side Waltz*. Her acclaimed performance in Michael Bennett's *Ballroom* earned her a nomination for another Tony Award.

REID SHELTON (Oliver Warbucks)

After a five-year run as the bald billionaire Daddy Warbucks—two-and-a-half years on Broadway in the role he originated at the Goodspeed Opera house and the rest on tour—Reid finally had a chance to let his hair grow in. "It's almost snow white, with streaks of blond in it," he exclaimed to a reporter. "Not having seen it for five years, I think it's gorgeous, and so does everybody else. I'm having great fun washing it and keeping it in shape."

But with or without hair, Reid's got a commanding presence and a heart of gold. "I don't know whether it's my look, personality, or what, but people have always thought that I've come from money," says Reid. "Actually, my family during the Depression was very poor."

But theater has enriched his life. "I'm terribly thrilled," he says, "when people come backstage and say, 'You made me cry.' I'm proud of that. If I can touch some

During a curtain call after Annie, *I'm flanked by original cast members (left to right) Sandy Faison, Reid Shelton, Sandy, Dorothy Loudon, Robert Fitch, and Raymond Thorne.* Ricky Ardis

response in people, and maybe open up something that they didn't even know they felt, that's a tremendous plus in being an actor."

Annie made his life a little easier, too. After his great reviews in the musical, Reid first considered moving from his rent-controlled apartment because the building was going downhill. But then he changed his mind. He bought the building.

Shaving his head twice a day was a small price to pay for his success in *Annie*, but he says it did alienate some people. For instance, Yul Brynner refused to be photographed with him. "Maybe he's afraid if the strobes hit our glistening heads simultaneously there will be no picture," he joked. When he ran into Yul on the street one day, he explained that he wasn't trying to copy him, but the part called for a bald Daddy Warbucks. Yul just laughed and said, "I know, I know. Congratulations."

Reid is better recognized with a full head of hair for his roles in a number of Broadway musicals. Among them: *The Rothschilds, Canterbury Tales, Oh, What A Lovely War, Wish You Were Here, My Fair Lady*, and *1600 Pennsylvania Avenue.*

He has also performed in revivals of *Carousel* at Lincoln Center and Jones Beach, and in off Broadway productions of *The Contractor, The Beggar's Opera*, and *Man with a Load of Mischief.*

On television, he has recently performed on CBS's *Tales of the Gold Monkey*; NBC's *Remington Steele, Cheers*, and *Knight Rider*; and an ABC pilot, *Too Good to Be True.*

BARBARA ERWIN (Lily)

Barbara began her professional career at age sixteen as a member of the famous Radio City Rockettes. After taking time away from the theater to raise five children, she came back to win wide recognition for her ability to play diverse roles.

For example, Barbara created the role of Lily in *Annie*, but she is also familiar to Broadway audiences as Martha in Michael Bennett's acclaimed production of *Ballroom* as well as for creating the roles of Hester and Kitty in *Animals.*

Barbara's portrayal of Gladys Bumps in the Chicago

production of *Pal Joey* brought her a nomination for a Joseph Jefferson Award. She also played Billy Dawn in *Born Yesterday* opposite Broderick Crawford.

Off Broadway, she appeared as Ruthie in *The Secret Life of Walter Mitty* and as Mazie in *Broadway*.

Television audiences may recognize her as Beulah on *One Life to Live* and as Madame Rosetta on *The Doctors*. Her film credits include *The Getaway* and *The Eyes of Laura Mars*.

Among her many other roles, she played Bonnie in *Anything Goes,* Joan in *Dames at Sea,* Gloria in *Everybody Loves Opal,* Gladys in *The Pajama Game,* and Lola in *Damn Yankees.*

LAURIE BEECHMAN (A Star to Be)

The role of A Star to Be was Laurie's first on Broadway, but she was already a well-known star on New York City's nightclub and cabaret circuit by the time she joined the Broadway cast of *Annie*. Laurie got her first taste of performing in 1971, when she attended New York University's School of the Arts. Afterward, she went on to become the featured vocalist in Cy Coleman's Men of Music concert at Hunter College. In addition to doing many radio jingles and voice-overs, Laurie has also performed in Shirley MacLaines' *Gypsy in My Soul*.

She has appeared at Reno Sweeney's, The Good Times, and Big Julie's to enthusiastic notices from audiences and critics alike. After *Annie*, Laurie moved to the cast of *Joseph and the Amazing Technicolor Dreamcoat*, where her performance earned her a Tony Award.

SANDY FAISON (Grace Farrell)

One week before *Annie* opened in New York, Sandy Faison still didn't know how she was going to portray

Grace Farrell. "They said, 'Do a Boston accent, do a British accent, do it any way you want.' " Once she found her character, however, she discovered she had other problems—like the time on stage when she grabbed Andrea McArdle's hand, only to find it full of already-chewed bubble gum.

Still, she says, "I've always liked kids and dogs. It's adults I have problems with. I'm loud; I talk too much. Kids don't mind if you're enthusiastic."

Sandy launched her professional career at age seventeen as Liza Minnelli's roommate in the *Sterile Cuckoo*. She has appeared off Broadway in *Pretzels*, where she sang and danced in nine different roles. Also, she created the role of Angie in *The Collected Works of Billy the Kid* in its American premiere at the Folger Theater. Her other theater appearances include the Syracuse Repertory's productions of *La Ronde; Finishing Touches*, with Celeste Holm and Barry Nelson; and *Lovers and Other Strangers*.

On TV, Sandy has performed in *Serpico* with David Birney, *Brenner* with Andy Griffith, and *Making It*, a TV pilot. She has studied and performed at Julliard and Chicago's Second City Improvisational Theatre.

Sandy says that she has hardly known a day without work, probably because she doesn't just sit around and wait for Broadway to call. "So you have to leave town for six weeks—big deal! I even love auditions. You can't give me enough of them. If you go up for enough of them, you're going to get something. That's what I call a working actor. I get a great sense of pride from it."

ROBERT FITCH (Rooster Hannigan)

Before drawing well-deserved hisses as the villainous con-artist Rooster Hannigan, Robert had already been in seventeen other Broadway productions, including *Mack and Mabel*, *Coco* with Katharine Hepburn, *Lorelei* with

Carol Channing, and *Promises, Promises.* He toured with Jerry Lewis in *Hellzapoppin* and starred in Playboy's *Bunnies '76.*

A member of the Helen Hayes Rep Company, he has played a number of Shakespearean roles and also has toured all over the world with Liza Minnelli's first act.

On TV, Robert performed in NBC's *Street of the Flowerboxes,* and ABC's *Norming of Jack 243.* The kids of *Annie* spent countless off stage hours watching Robert weave through a wondrous routine of magic tricks.

RAYMOND THORNE (FDR)

Annie's FDR, Raymond Thorne has also been in New York productions of *Dames at Sea, Man with a Load of Mischief, The Magistrate, The Wedding, Rose,* and *The Knight of Olmedo.*

In regional productions, he has played the role of Rutledge in *1776* at Houston's Theatre Under the Stars. In addition, he's performed in a number of roles at the Washington Theatre Club and at the Cincinnati Playhouse in the Park.

And that's not all for this versatile and active actor: Raymond has appeared in the touring company of *Applause* with Lauren Bacall, *Never Too Late* with Imogene Coca, and *Seidman and Son* with Menasha Skulnick. Also, he has performed in *Born Yesterday, Critic's Choice, Angel Street,* and *The Importance of Being Earnest.*

Raymond's television credits before *Annie* included performances on *Love of Life, All My Children* and *The Defenders.*

SANDY (Himself)

"He's the Laurence Olivier of dogs," says Sandy's trainer, Bill Berloni, who plucked him from certain death at a Connecticut pound in 1976 in a desperate search for a canine star for *Annie*. What set Sandy apart from 300 other dogs he surveyed, says Bill, was his aristocratic temperament: "He was the only one who was not jumping up and down and making noise."

Sandy, a mutt whose relatives were most likely Airdales and Irish wolfhounds, was an instant hit the minute Bill showed him to Martin Charnin, who was readying *Annie* for its opening at the Goodspeed Opera House. No matter that the eighteen-month old dog was thought to have been an abused pet. There was something about his floppy ears, shaggy hair, and cowering manner that seemed to signal stardom.

At any rate, it took two months for Bill, an actor and technical assistant at Goodspeed, to train Sandy for the show. He says he did it by showering Sandy with love and by letting him hang around the stage, where he got to know the cast and crew. Then, finally, he taught him his "lines"—how to crawl to Annie onstage, lie quietly for a while, run to her when she calls to him, and leave the stage when the policemen take Annie back to the orphanage.

Sandy learned his lessons so well that by the time the show got to Broadway, his role had actually expanded. From that time on, he received royal treatment. He traveled in limousines, dined at the White House at a black-tie dinner, and as Bill Berloni put it in *Pet News*: "He gets an ovation from the audience even when he misses a cue." He even had an understudy—a dog named Arf Bill found in a pound in New York City and trained as he had Sandy.

These days, Sandy has "retired" to a rustic lakeside retreat in New Jersey, where Bill Berloni contemplates offers of commercials and even a lecture tour for his famous pet.

PRODUCTION STAFF

MARTIN CHARNIN (Director/Lyricist)

Martin, as the creator, lyricist, director, and ultimate cheerleader for the show, was the "Big Daddy" of the *Annie* company. He started his professional career in show business as an actor in the original production of *West Side Story*. During the show's New York run he played the part of Big Deal and sang the memorable, "Gee, Officer Krupke."

It was while he was in *West Side Story* that he first started writing lyrics, and he went on to write on Broadway for *Hot Spot, Zenda* and to collaborate with Richard Rodgers on *Two by Two*, a musical about Noah and the Flood, which starred Danny Kaye. He conceived and directed *Nash at Nine* with E. G. Marshall and also created, with Alan Jay Lerner, *Music, Music*, a history of the American musical theater.

"I think I'm a terrific lyricist," Martin told a reporter in the wake of *Annie's* success. "But I'm not a fancy lyricist." Some of his ideas, he says, are simple: He came up with the idea for "N.Y.C."—the ode to New York City in Act I of *Annie*—while sitting at his desk staring at a subway token!

In essence, Martin is a one-man theatrical powerhouse, and his output over the years has been staggering. His music and lyrics for "The Best Thing You've Ever Done," written for Barbra Streisand, earned him a gold record. He's produced and directed supper-club acts for such stars as Leslie Uggams and Dionne Warwick. He's also done a spate of television spectaculars, including the Emmy Award-winning TV special *Annie: The Women in the Life of a Man* starring Anne Bancroft; and *'S Wonder-*

ful, 'S Marvelous, 'S Gershwin starring Jack Lemmon and Fred Astaire, which won him two Emmys and a Peabody Award for broadcasting.

But he hasn't stopped there. One of his recent hits was a cabaret-style revue, *Upstairs at O'Neals,* modeled after the famous Upstairs-Downstairs revues Julius Monk popularized in the fifties. Another Broadway venture, *The First,* a musical about the life of baseball's Jackie Robinson, didn't get to first base on Broadway but scored with the critics, earning Martin two Tony nominations.

"What I'd really like is to have five musicals running on Broadway at once," Martin once told a theater critic. "Like a juggler who spins fifty plates in the air at once. In theory, the first plate has got to get a long spin so it's still going when the fiftieth gets there. Fortunately, my number one spin's going to sit there for a good long time."

THOMAS MEEHAN (Author)

When a reporter once told Thomas Meehan that it was hard to believe that *Annie* was the first show he ever wrote, the author said, "I know. Sometimes I don't believe it, either. Sometimes I don't believe it at all."

Well, by now he should believe it! Thanks to *Annie's* success, Tom claims that he was able to open his first savings account in years. Perhaps a Broadway story in itself, Tom's career had not exactly been one of unbounded success. "Somebody asked me, 'What are you going to do after *Annie* opens?' And I said, 'If it fails, I'm going up the highway and jump off the George Washington Bridge.' "

But at this point he says, "What's worrying me now is that there's nothing to worry about."

Formerly a staff writer for the *New Yorker,* Tom was well known for his humorous short pieces. In addition to contributing to more than twenty magazines, he was nominated for an Emmy Award for his satirical sketches for TV's *That Was the Week That Was*. *Annie* was his first try at the theater, and his work won him a Tony and a Drama Desk Award.

CHARLES STROUSE (Composer)

Charles is the source of the music for a string of successful Broadway productions, including *Bye, Bye Birdie* and *Applause*, for which he won Tony Awards. He took home a third Tony for *Annie*. He has also written the scores for several films and television productions, including *Bonnie and Clyde* and the theme song for *All in the Family*.

PETER GENNARO (Choreographer)

Peter's "dazzling" choreography for *Annie* brought audiences to their feet time and time again. That was no surprise, however, because he'd had years of performing and choreographing experience on Broadway as well as for television. He has produced shows at Radio City Music Hall, and was co-choreographer of *West Side Story*.

For his work on *Annie*, Peter took home a Tony Award and a Drama Desk Award.

Before joining *Annie*, he choreographed *Fiorello!*, *The Unsinkable Molly Brown*, *Bajour*, and *Irene*, among many others. He has also performed in nightclubs in New York and Las Vegas.

THEONI V. ALDREDGE (Costume Designer)

Thanks to Theoni, the Academy Award winning designer for the *The Great Gatsby*, *Annie* was a comic book look-alike, down to her white-collared red dress and Mary-Jane style shoes. But the orphans' baggy dresses and high-top lace-up shoes were purely imaginary, the product of the design talent that has created the costumes for nearly 100 Broadway and off-Broadway shows.

Theoni's costumes for *Annie* won her a Tony Award and a Drama Desk Award. She followed up this triumph by winning a second Tony for *Barnum*, and by designing the fabulous clothes in the Broadway hits *42nd Street* and *Dreamgirls*.

Since 1960, Theoni has been the principal designer for the New York Shakespeare Festival.

PHILIP LANG (Orchestration)

As orchestrator for *Annie*, Philip brought years of experience and outstanding success with a variety of Broadway shows such as *My Fair Lady*, *Annie Get Your Gun*, *Camelot*, *Applause*, and *Carnival*.

PETER HOWARD (Musical Director & Dance Music Arranger)

A noted dance music arranger who has worked in such Broadway hits as *Chicago*, *Carnival* and *The Roar of the Greasepaint*, Peter is best known for his work as music director and arranger for *Hello, Dolly!* and *1776*. Before Annie, he also served as Music Director for the annual Milliken Breakfast Shows.

DAVID MITCHELL (Scene Designer)

You may never see him, but you'll see his work. One reviewer (Rex Reed) referred to his sets as "a feast for the eyes." In addition to his work as the ingenious scene designer for *Annie*, David has long worked with the New York Shakespeare Festival, designing the sets for their productions of *Henry V, Mrs. Warren's Profession,* and *Trelawny of the "Wells."* David's work on *Short Eyes* won him a Drama Desk Award.

His other work includes *The Incomparable Max, Steambath, Colette, How the Other Half Loves, I Love My Wife,* and *The Gin Game.* He has also designed sets for the major opera houses throughout the country, including the New York City Opera, and the San Francisco, Washington and Houston Opera Companies. His designs for *Annie* earned David the Tony Award and the Outer Critics' Circle Award.